The Last Shot

Essays on Civil War Politics,
the Demise of John Wilkes Booth,
and the Republican Myth
of the Assassinated Lincoln

William L. Richter
&
J. E. "Rick" Smith, III

The Last Shot
Essays on Civil War Politics, the Demise of John Wilkes Booth, and the Republican Myth of the Assassinated Lincoln

Copyright © 2016 William L. Richter and J. E. "Rick" Smith. All rights reserved. No part of this book may be reproduced or retransmitted in any form or by any means without the written permission of the publisher.

Published by Wheatmark®
1760 East River Road, Suite 145, Tucson, Arizona 85718 USA
www.wheatmark.com

ISBN: 978-1-62787-355-0
LCCN: 2015953611

Contents

ACKNOWLEDGEMENTS
v

PREFACE
History Is Written by Those
Who Have Hanged the Heroes
1

I. "PULLING DOWN THE COLOSSUS"
John Wilkes Booth, America's First Successful
Presiden
tial Assassin
7

II. "DELIBERATELY AND PERSONALLY CONCEIVED"
Did Abraham Lincoln and the
Republicans Intentionally
Cause the Civil War?
26

III. GEORGE N. SANDERS
A Professional Revolutionary for Manifest Destiny,
an Independent Confederacy, and
Worldwide Constitutional Government
55

IV. GUS HOWELL
Smarmy, Arrogant Blockade Runner and Murderer,
or Effective-Behind-the-Lines Confederate Operative?
76

V. Isaac in Texas
A Theoretical Look at the Other Surratt
87

VI. "I Don't Really Know What to Make of It"
The Owens Statement, the Survival of Booth's Horses,
and the Move to the Potomac
97

VII. "I Told Him He Must Go Away"
Elizabeth Rousby Quesenberry
and the Escape of Lincoln's Assassin
108

VIII. "Behold! I Tell You a Mystery"
Who Was Mr. Crismond?
115

IX. "I Shall Shoot Myself Through the Head"
Could John Wilkes Booth Have Committed
Suicide at Garrett's Farm?
122

X. Why Couldn't We Have Gotten
an American for the Job?
Congressional Supremacy, the Radical Republicans,
and the Impeachment of Andrew Johnson
134

Acknowledgements

Many thanks to the following persons:

Director Laurie Verge and Librarian Sandra Walia, of the Surratt Museum in Clinton, Maryland, for their never-ending, good-natured assistance and encouragement.

Nicholas Scheetz, head of the Georgetown University Library Special Collections Division; Scott S. Taylor, Manuscripts Processor; Kristina Bobe, Librarian, Government Documents and Microforms Department; and Chris Ulrich, Library Assistant; at Georgetown University Libraries, Lauinger Library.

The over-worked staff at the Inter-Library Loan desk of the University of Arizona, which kept us supplied with numerous, obscure sources from obscure collections.

Special thanks goes to Betty Ownsby for designing the cover, and making numerous suggestions to improving the manuscript layout, and to Lynne Richter for making the manuscript ready for the printer.

We thank you one and all. The credit for this volume goes to you.

Preface

HISTORY IS WRITTEN BY THOSE WHO HAVE HANGED THE HEROES[1]

On December 20, 1860, with the secession of South Carolina from the Union, the Unites States died.[2] At least, the American Republic, represented by the Founding Fathers, the Declaration of Independence of 1776, the Articles of Confederation of 1781, and the Constitution of 1787, perished.

But that is not the story modern Americans know. Instead, we are taught that the fraud of secession and the sham of the Confederacy were defeated by the noble President Abraham Lincoln, and the Union was saved through a New Birth of Freedom. Then, at the hour of his triumph, Lincoln's personal victory was spoiled with his assassination by a mentally unbalanced actor and Southern sympathizer, John Wilkes Booth.

But what if the "accepted" story is wrong? What if President Lincoln's modern reputation is a Yankee fabrication to justify an unjust war? What if John Wilkes Booth were not merely a misguided racist? What if he were not the craziest of what historian and family biographer Stanley Kimmel once called the "Mad Booths of Maryland." What if John Wilkes Booth and those who stood behind him were rational men?

This different history of Lincoln is really nothing new.

---
1 Robert the Bruce in the voice-over introduction to the movie *Braveheart* (1995).
2 Akhil Amar Reed, *The Law of the Land: A Grand Tour of Our Constitutional Republic* (New York: Basic Books, 2015), 3-4.

John Wilkes Booth was deeply aware of it, but it goes against the Republican Myth of the Assassinated Lincoln that passes for history today. Alphonso Taft, future U.S. Secretary of War (1876), U.S. Attorney General (1876-1877), and nineteenth century progenitor of the family that produced a slew of noted, modern Ohio Republican politicians, understood what changes had to take place.

Anticipating the themes of modern commentators, Taft wrote about the necessities of future history in a letter to his home-state U.S. solon, Senator *pro tem* Benjamin Wade, on September 8, 1864:

> It is to be regretted that history should have to tell so many lies as it will tell, when it shall declare Lincoln's intrigues and foolishness models of integrity and wisdom, his weakened and wavering indecision and delay farsighted statesmanship, and his blundering usurpation of legislative power Jacksonian courage and Roman patriotism, but one cannot help it. History goes with the powers that be.[3]

The success of the historical spin of the Lincolnites (defined by one disgruntled critic as "those empowered to tell the rest of us rubes what everything really means") would please Alphonso Taft and puzzle John Wilkes Booth were they to be resurrected to modern America. Present-day historians regularly vote Abraham Lincoln as one of the top three presidents in the nation's history, usually number one.

The ten essays which encompass this book invite you, the reader, to suspend your belief, if only for a few moments, in the

---

3   The copy of the letter from Alfonso Taft to Ben Wade is from the David Rankin Barbee Papers, Box 3, Archives, Georgetown University.

"traditional view" of American history and to look at the Republican Myth of the Assassinated Lincoln from a new and different perspective.

The first essay reveals John Wilkes Booth as an ordinary Southerner, very much a man of his time, holding to a cooperationist political philosophy, which was very common in the South before the Civil War. The second study asks whether Lincoln and the Republicans intentionally started the Civil War to bring about the end of slavery. Neither has been printed before.

The third piece brings forth George N. Sanders, the one true revolutionary in the Southern quest for independence. It has appeared before[4]. The fourth essay examines Gus Howell, a shadowy figure who first served the Confederate army and then the secret service. It, too, has been printed earlier.[5]

The fifth piece looks at Isaac Surratt, the older brother of the better-known John H Surratt, Jr., who fought his war in Texas along the Rio Grande. It has appeared earlier[6]. The sixth essay questions the established tale of Thomas Jones keeping Booth and Herold in seclusion and assisting in their arrival at the Potomac. It has never been in print before.

The seventh piece is a look at Mrs. Elizabeth Quesenberry, who provided food, delivered by Rebel agent Thomas Harbin, who assisted Booth and Herold on their way. It was first published in 2008.[7] The eighth essay is a study of the seldom-mentioned man who took Booth to a Confederate safe house in Virginia. It also has appeared before.[8]

---

4 J. E. "Rick" Smith, III, and Willian L. Richter, "George N. Sanders," SURRATT COURIER, 37 (February 2012), 3-12.
5 *Id.* and *id., ibid.,* "Gus Howell," 36 (September 2011), 3-8. See also, the home page to Randal Berry's forum, lincoln-assassination.com.
6 *Id.* and *id., ibid.,* "Isaac in Texas," 33 (November 2008), 3-7.
7 *Id* and *id.,* ibid., "Quesenberry," 33 (September 2008), 4-7.
8 *Id.* and *id.,* ibid., "Crismond," 38 (March 2013), 11-14.

The ninth paper theorizes whether Booth could have committed suicide at Garrett's Locust Hill Farm, contrary to the time honored account of his dying at the hands of Sgt. Thomas "Boston" Corbett. It has been printed twice before.[9]

The final study looks at what the Republican Party was trying to achieve politically in its quarrels with Presidents Lincoln and Johnson throughout the throes of Civil War and Reconstruction. It has never appeared in print before.

The Republican Myth of the Assassinated Lincoln bridges a unique gap in American history. In reality, there are two Americas—there is the United States before Lincoln (typified by the phrase "the United States *are*"), a federal republic guaranteed by the written Constitution, and the United States after Lincoln (typified by the phrase "the United States *is*"), an empire under a "living" Constitution, that means nothing more than the current generation of the ruling class says it does.

Under the empire that Lincoln and the Republican Party created with their victory at Appomattox by defeating the once dominant Old South, the new United States went forth to conquer the American West, "civilize" Asia and the Caribbean, and subdue the world with its industrial production enhanced by American victories in two World Wars and numerous police actions that destroyed our enemies and allies alike. Not until the tragedies of Viet Nam and the assassination of President John F. Kennedy did Abraham Lincoln's American empire know defeat.[10]

---

9 First in three parts as *id.* and *id.*, "Booth Bombshell: Not Suicide by Cop," February 10, 2012, Suite 101.com, under the editorship of Rick Stelnick and in the *Surratt Courier*, "I Shall Shoot Myself," 38 (May 2013), pp. 3-8, under the editorship of Laurie Verge.

10 The concept of the American growth to world power is a theme from Victor Davis Hanson, "Presidents Aren't What They Used to Be," July 16, 2009, Jewish World Review. com/0709/hanson071609.php3. For the South as an exception to the rule of progress, see C. Vann Woodward, "The Irony of Southern History," *Journal of Southern History*, 19 (1953), 3-19.

Admittedly, there were setbacks here and there.[11] They were especially notable every twenty years, like clockwork starting in 1840, marring the seemingly inevitable American march of progress. These were the sudden deaths of seven presidents, three from natural causes, and four more, beginning with Lincoln, from violence. This alleged curse of Tecumseh's brother, the Shawnee Prophet, on President William Henry Harrison for politically profiting from the 1811 Battle of Tippecanoe and those who followed him each decade into office, seems to have been broken by Ronald W. Reagan's survival of an assassination attempt in 1981 and George W. Bush's presidency, unmarred by assassination endeavors, that followed in 2000.

So come with us then back to those Elysian days just before and after Appomattox, when the United States was still a republic—to a time before it became an empire—to that brief moment before its history was told by those who hanged the heroes, literally and figuratively, with the Republican Myth of the Assassinated Lincoln.

---

11 Some of these problems are discussed in C. Vann Woodward, "A Second Look at the Theme of Irony," in Woodward (ed.), *The Burden of Southern History* (New York: Mentor, 1969, rev. ed.), 150–62.

I.

"Pulling Down the Colossus"

John Wilkes Booth, America's First Successful Presidential Assassin

According to legend, fifteen-year-old John Wilkes Booth and his boyhood school chums attending St. Timothy's Academy at Catonsville, Maryland, in the mid-1850s, were resting on the drill field one day during a break in their training.. Despite its religious-sounding name, St. Timothy's was a privately run military school, where the gray-uniformed cadets regularly practiced company-sized close order infantry maneuvers. Dismissed from formation after a tiring drill, the students sat down beneath the shade trees that lined the field and chatted about their futures and what they hoped to achieve in life.

Some hoped to be great lawyers and politicians, bigger than Daniel Webster or even renowned local Maryland hero, Reverdy Johnson. Others had similar aspirations in different fields of endeavor. But the normally boisterous Johnny Booth stood by and said little.

"What do you want to do in life, Billy Bow-legs?" one student inquired finally, using Booth's school nickname (they all had one). Booth relished his sobriquet because it belonged to a fierce Seminole Seminole chief who had fought for his people's freedom against the U.S. government.

"I hope to do something big, really big," Johnny said. "Something like pulling down the Colossus of Rhodes!"

"What?" came the rejoinder. "That thing was destroyed by an earthquake over two thousand years ago!"

"Yeah. But wouldn't it be great? Suppose that statue was now standing, and I should by some means overthrow it? My name would descend to posterity and never be forgotten, for it would be in all the histories of the times, and be read thousands of years after we are dead, and no matter how smart and good men we may be, we would never get our names in so many histories!"

"But suppose the falling statue took you down with it? Then where would all your glory be?"

"I should die with the satisfaction of knowing I had done something never before accomplished by any other man, and something no other man would do."[12]

Although neither he nor his schoolmates realized it then, Johnny Booth had unwittingly become a prophet.[13] And for ful-

---

12 On Booth's education, such as it was, see Terry Alford (ed.), *John Wilkes Booth: A Sister's Memoir by Asia Booth Clarke* (Jackson: University Press of Mississippi, 1996), 31-101, *passim*; James O. Hall, "John Wilkes Booth at School," *Surratt Courier*, 16 (July 1991), 3-4; John Rhodehamel and Louise Taper (eds.), *"Right or Wrong, God Judge Me": The Writings of John Wilkes Booth* (Urbana: University of Illinois Press, 1997), 37n.1; Theodore Roscoe, *Web of Conspiracy* (Englewood Cliffs, N.J.: Prentice-Hall, 1959), 32-33.

John Wilkes Booth was as bow-legged as his father (Rhodehamel and Taper [eds.], *The Writings of John Wilkes Booth*, 38n.1) and, unbeknownst to him, he shared the boyhood sobriquet "Billy Bow-legs" with none other than Lincoln's secretary of State, William H. Seward. See Shelby Foote, *The Civil War* (3 vols., New York: Vintage Press, 1974), I, 18.

13 An essential place to start any examination of John Wilkes Booth is Blaine V. Houmes, *Abraham Lincoln Assassination Bibliography: A Compendium of Reference Materials* (Clinton, Md.: Surratt Society, 1997). The most recent scholarly biography is Terry Alford, *Fortune's Fool: The Life of John Wilkes Booth* (NewYork: Oxford, 2015). But see, Constance Head, "John Wilkes Booth in American Fiction," *Lincoln Herald*, 82 (Winter 1980), 455-62; and her "John Wilkes Booth as a Hero Figure, "*Journal of American Culture*, 5 (Fall 1982), 22-28, who argues that a fictional account might allow the reader reach the real Booth, in a manner non-fiction never can. This point is argued without reference to Booth in Jill Lepore, "Just the Facts, Ma'am: Fake Memoirs, Factual Fictions, and the History of History," *The New Yorker*, 83 (March 24, 2008), 79-83. For a sample of Boothian fiction, consult Steven G. Miller, "John Wilkes Booth and the Lincoln Assassination in Recent Fiction," *Surratt Courier*, 29 (June 2004), 4-9, which lists twenty-nine pieces of fiction from the period 1983 to 2003 alone. For the complete tale of Booth and his associates in the format of historical fiction, see William L. Richter, *The Last Confederate Heroes: The Final Struggle for Southern Independence & the Assassination of Abraham Lincoln* (3rd Ed., Tucson, Az.: Wheatmark, 2014).

filling this augury Booth would become one of the most vilified persons in American history—known to generations of Americans as the quintessential radical, the first successful presidential assassin or, in the measured words of biographer Philip Van Doren Stern, as "the man who killed Lincoln."[14]

Another historian of the Booth family went Stern one step further. Stanley Kimmel referred to John Wilkes Booth, in the words of a common nineteenth condemnation, as the craziest of the "Mad Booths of Maryland." Brother Edwin tried to shift all the blame for the family's oddities to Johnny's shoulders, saying that Johnny "was a rattle-pated fellow, filled with Quixotic notions." But fellow actor Edwin Forrest bluntly summed up the public verdict after the assassination of Abraham Lincoln, when he stated, "*All* those goddam Booths were crazy."[15]

Despite their well-known eccentricities (and every family member had at least one), the Booths were far from insane. This was especially true of the allegedly craziest Booth of them all, John Wilkes.[16] Born the ninth of ten siblings, Johnny was un-

---

[14] Philip Van Doren Stern, *The Man Who Killed Lincoln: The Story of John Wilkes Booth and His Part in the Assassination* (New York: Literary Guild of America, Inc., 1939). Booth was not the first man to attempt to assassinate a U.S. president. Richard Lawrence tried to kill Andrew Jackson in 1835 in the rotunda of the capitol, but both of his pistols misfired. As with all future presidential assassins, or would-be assassins, Lawrence was immediately declared insane—and probably was. See Robert V. Remini, *Andrew Jackson and the Course of American Democracy, 1933-1845* (Harper & Row, 1984), 228-29.

[15] Edwin Booth to Nahum Capen, July 28th, 1881, in Stern, *Man Who Killed Lincoln*, 396-97. See also, Stanley Kimmel, *The Mad Booths of Maryland* (2nd ed., rev. and enlarged, New York: Dover Publications, 1969), Forrest quote from 290. On Americans liking their presidential assassins to be insane, see James W. Clarke, "Conspiracies, Myths, and the Will to Believe: The Importance of Context," in Gabor S. Boritt and Norman O. Forness (eds.), *The Historian's Lincoln: Pseudohistory, Psychohistory, and History* (Urbana: University of Illinois Press, 1988), 365-73.

[16] The perennial interest in Booth is explored in Gene Smith, "The Booth Obsession," *American Heritage*, 52 (September 1992), 105-19. Besides Alford, *Fortune's Fool*, nonfiction treatments of Booth include, Francis Wilson, *John Wilkes Booth: Fact and Fiction of Lincoln's Assassination* (Boston: Houghton Mifflin, 1929); David Balsiger and Charles E. Sellier, Jr., *The Lincoln Conspiracy* (Los Angeles: Schick Sunn Classic Productions, 1977); Thomas R. Turner, *Beware the People Weeping: Public Opinion and the Assassination of Abraham Lincoln* (Baton Rouge: Louisiana State University Press, 1982), and his more recent *The Assassination of Abraham Lincoln* (Malabar, Fl.: Krieger Publishing Co., 1999); William Hanchett, *The Lincoln Murder Conspiracies* (Urbana: University of Illinois Press,

doubtedly the most spoiled boy of his day. His mother doted on the handsome child with the alabaster skin, dark eyes, and wavy, coal-black hair. His winning personality, wide-eyed innocence, and loving embrace won over his brothers, sisters, and childhood friends alike. The untimely death of his father, just as Johnny entered his teenage years, gave the often ill-disciplined boy a devil-may-care outlook on the world.

Although his school performance was not always up to par, modern Americans often forget that Johnny was well educated for his time. Moreover, his acting led to a lot of reading and memorizing of the complexity of William Shakespeare's tales of Tudor civic intrigue and did much to widen his own political horizons as Americans marched toward secession and civil war. This is aptly demonstrated in his search for a rationale of his actions before and during the War for Southern Independence.[17]

Booth's changing political positions are revealed in his own

1983); William A Tidwell, with James O. Hall and David Winfred Gaddy, *Come Retribution: The Confederate Secret Service and the Assassination of Lincoln* (Jackson: University Press of Mississippi, 1988), William A Tidwell,. *April '65: Confederate Covert Action in the Civil War* (Kent, Ohio: The Kent State University Press, 1995); Richard Bak, *The Day Lincoln Was Shot: An Illustrated Chronicle* (Dallas: Taylor Publishing Company, 1998); Steers, *Blood on the Moon* (2001); Jay Winik, *April 1865: The Month that Saved America* (New York: HarperCollins, 2001; Leonard F. Guttridge and Ray A. Neff, *Dark Union: The Secret Web of Profiteers, Politicians, and Booth Conspirators that Led to Lincoln's Death* (Hoboken, N.J.: Weilet, 2003); H. Donald Winkler, *Lincoln and Booth: More Light on the Conspiracy* (Nashville: Cumberland House, 2003); Michael W. Kauffman, *American Brutus: John Wilkes Booth and the Lincoln Conspiracies* (New York: Random House, 2004); Higham, Charles. *Murdering Mr. Lincoln: A New Detection of the Nineteenth Century's Most Famous Crime* (Beverly Hills: New Mellenium Press, 2004); James L. Swanson, *Manhunt: The 12-Day Chase for Lincoln's Killer* (New York: HarperCollins, 2006).

17   For a study of Booth's political views, see William L. Richter, *Sic Semper Tyrannis: Why John Wilkes Booth Shot Abraham Lincoln* (Bloomington, Ind.: iUniverse, 2009). Booth's place in history is established in William Hanchett, *John Wilkes Booth and the Terrrible Truth About the Civil War* (Racine: Lincoln Fellowship of Wisconsin. Historical Bulletin No. 49. Psychological forays into the mind of Booth include, Francis Wilson, *John Wilkes Booth*; Constance Head, "J.W.B.: I am Myself Alone," in Michael W. Kauffman (ed.), *In Pursuit of . . . : Continuing Research in the Field of the Lincoln Assassination* (Clinton, Md.: Surratt Society, 1990), 41-46; Philip Weissman, "Why Booth Killed Lincoln: A Psychoanalytic Study," *Psychoanalysis and the Social Sciences*, 5 (1958), 99-11; George W. Wilson, "John Wilkes Booth: Father Murderer," *American Imago*, 1 (1940), 49-60; Barbara Lerner, "The Killer Narcissists," *National Review On-line*, May 19, 1999, at townhall.com; and Christopher New, *America's Civil War*, March 1993, at erols.com/candidus/wilkes-1.

papers collected by John Rhodehamel and Louise Taper in their fine volume, *"Right or Wrong, God Judge Me": The Writings of John Wilkes Booth*. A careful analysis of Booth's writings reveals that he skillfully shifted his Civil War era political positions in three key documents from Constitutional Unionist to Secessionist to Tyrannicide as the war progressed.

Booth's first statement of political values is his never-delivered Philadelphia speech of December 1860, often called the "Allow Me" speech from its first words. Historians have tried to analyze this 5,000 word Philippic (the longest single statement of Booth's beliefs) three times before.[18] They see it as a racist, pro-slavery reprise of Marc Anthony's "question and answer litany" from Shakespeare's Julius Caesar that revolved around the reserved powers to the states guaranteed in the Tenth Amendment to the U.S. Constitution.[19] All this may be true, but it misses Booth's actual meaning hidden in his often-wordy bombast.

What then was Booth's political philosophy in 1860? Modern American students quickly and erroneously answer, states' rights. But like most prewar pro-slave thinkers, Booth abhorred states' rights. "I never could understand this sectional feeling," Booth asserted. "True, in time of peace it may be a blessing, as it stimulates a generous rivalry to make our country great. But in times like these it is a heavy curse.... We are all one people," Booth said, "the whole Union is our country."[20]

---

18 Rhodehamel and Taper (eds.), *Writings of John Wilkes Booth*, 47-69, including analysis, and Jeannine Clarke Dodels, "Water on Stone: A Study of John Wilkes Booth's 1860 Political Draft Preserved at the Players' Club NY," copy in hands of the author and her "John Wilkes Booth's Secession Crisis Speech of 1860" in Arthur Kincaid (ed.), *John Wilkes Booth, Actor: The Proceedings of a Conference Weekend in Bel Air, Maryland, May 1988* (North Leigh, Oxfordshire: Privately Published, 1988), 48-51.

19 Dodels, "Water on Stone," 18 (question and answer); Dodels, "John Wilkes Booth's Secession Crisis Speech of 1860," in Kincaid (ed.), *John Wilkes Booth, Actor*, 49 (reserved powers); Rhodehamel and Taper (eds.), *Writings of John Wilkes Booth*, 52-53.

20 Rhodehamel and Taper (eds.), *Writings of John Wilkes Booth*, 56-57.

How about secession? Surely Booth was a secessionist. But hear him once again: "I will not fight for secession. No, I will not fight for disunion. . . . I don't mean to admit that the South should secede nor do I believe a state can secede without revolution & blood-shed."[21]

What, then did Booth want? "I am a northern man," Booth admitted. "But I will fight with all my heart and soul, even if there is not a man to back me, for equal rights and justice to the South. . . . The South wants justice, has waited for it long and she will wait no longer," Booth said. "I would not have you violate our country's laws. . . . But I could wish you would prove to the South, with deeds, instead of words, that she shall have those rights which she demands, *those rights which are her due.*"[22]

The rights Booth referred to were the South's claims to the so-called "Peculiar Institution" or slavery. "Much, too much, has been said on that subject," Booth conceded. "I'll touch [on] it lightly. . . . First, I know that the South has a right according to the Constitution to keep and hold [slaves]," Booth said, "and we have no right under that Constitution to interfere with her or hers."[23]

Booth was aware that everyone, North or South, recognized that slavery could not be abolished in the United States without a constitutional amendment passed by three-fourths of the states. As the slave-holding South comprised around half of the states throughout the antebellum period, no amendment would succeed.[24]

But Booth went on from the usual superficial assertion to

---

21 *Ibid.*, 55, 61.

22 *Ibid.*, 55, 57.

23 *Ibid.*, 62.

24 For the South's prewar power in national politics, see Leonard L. Richards, *The Slave Power: The Free North and Southern Domination* (Baton Rouge: Louisiana State University Press, 2000). See also, William L. Richter, "Introduction," in his *Historical Dictionary of the Old South* (Lanham, Md.: Scarecrow Press, 2006), 1-29.

hold slaves to another topic of greater importance. This was the recognition of certain extraterritorial rights that attached to slaveholding in the Constitution of 1787 through the so-called Fugitive Clause (Article 4, Section 2, Clause 3). What the South held, and Booth agreed with, basically, was that slaveholding states were justified in controlling the internal policies of non-slaveholding states through the actions of the federal government whenever those policies adversely affected, even indirectly, the institution of slavery. This was the essence of extraterritoriality.[25]

At this point in his presentation, Booth suddenly left off writing and never finished or delivered his speech. But before quitting, he referred to the two major constitutional issues of extraterritoriality that preceded and helped cause the Civil War, the advance of slavery into the territories, and the pursuit and return of fugitive slaves to their owners.

"What rights have you to exclude [S]outhern rights from the ter[r]itor[ies]? [B]ecause you are the strongest?" Booth asked, in response to Republican criticism of the U.S. Supreme Court decision (by a vote of 7 to 2) in the recent case, Dred Scott

---

25 Arthur Bestor, "State Sovereignty and Slavery: A Reinterpretation of Pro-slavery Constitutional Doctrine, 1846-1860," Illinois State Historical Society, *Journal*, 53 (1960), 117-27.

It was this definition of extraterritoriality that caused Abraham Lincoln to give his "House Divided" speech (Roy P. Basler [ed.], *The Collected Works of Abraham Lincoln* [9 vols., New Brunswick, N.J.: Rutgers University Press, 1953-1955], II, 461-69), maintaining, after the writings of pro-slave thinker George Fitzhugh of Port Royal, Virginia, that a nation could not endure half-slave and half-free, but soon must become one or the other. See Eugene D. Genovese, *The World the Slaveholders Made: Two Essays in Interpretation* (New York: Vantage Books, 1971), 118, *passim*.

This has caused others to accuse Lincoln of starting the Civil War because he believed that he needed to short-cut a New York Case, Lemmon v. People, making the right of transit in slaves permanent (i.e., making slavery legal throughout the U.S.) so long as the owner did not assume citizenship in the free state, from reaching the U.S. Supreme Court. See Alexander Gigante, "Slavery and a House Divided," at http://afroamhistory.about.com/library/prm/blhousedivided.htm; Paul Finkelman, "The Nationalization of Slavery: A Counter-factual Approach to the 1860s," *Louisiana Studies*, 14 (Fall 1975), 213-40, especially 221-33. See also, James M. McPherson, "What Caused the Civil War?" *North & South*, 4 (November 2000), 12-22; Jeffrey R. Hummel, "Why Did Lincoln Choose War?" *ibid.*, 4 (September 2001), 38-44; Webb Garrison, *Lincoln's Little War* (Nashville: Rutledge Hill Press, 1997).

v. Sanford (1857). "I have as much right to carry my slave into the ter[r]itor[ies] as you have to carry your paid servant or your children."[26]

In this, Booth and the Supreme Court supported the Southern-inspired Non-Exclusion Doctrine that had been a key part of the Democratic Party's platform in 1848. Introduced by Alabamian William L. Yancey at the 1848 Presidential Nominating Convention, this plank stated that slave property could not be kept out of the territories of the United States because under the Constitution of 1787, through the fugitive clause, a Southern state's slave law adhered to the chattel no matter where he or she went until freed by positive action of one's master.[27]

Booth then mentioned "[t]he fugitive slave law," which Congress had passed ten tears earlier as part of the Compromise of 1850.[28] What Booth was referring to here was not criminal extradition, which under the Constitution of 1787 could be denied by one state to another (Article 4, Section 2, Clause 2). He was noting the absolute right of recaption of labor fugitives, or slaves (Article 4, Section 2, Clause 3, since obliterated by the Thirteenth Amendment).[29]

The U.S. Supreme Court had upheld recaption of runaway labor in 1842 (Prigg v. Pennsylvania, by a 6 to 1 vote) and 1859 (Ableman v. Booth, by a unanimous 9 to 0 vote), despite the numerous attempts of free states to nullify and their citizens to disobey the Federal fugitive slave acts of 1790 and 1850 through state-passed Personal Liberty laws.[30]

---

26 Rhodehamel and Taper (eds.), *Writings of John Wilkes Booth*, 64.

27 Bestor, "State Sovereignty and Slavery," 147-62, for a discussion of slavery in the territories.

28 Rhodehamel and Taper (eds.), *Writings of John Wilkes Booth*, 64.

29 Bestor, "State Sovereignty and Slavery," 130-40, for the fugitive problem in all of its manifestations.

30 Richter, *Sic Semper Tyrannis*, 101-113, for the fugitive cases.

With active support like this from the National government on behalf of slavery, Booth correctly saw no need for secession in 1861, even after the election of Lincoln threatened that support. "No, no!" thundered Booth. "This Union must and shall be preserved," he bellowed, echoing the words of President Andrew Jackson during the first secession (Nullification) crisis nearly thirty years earlier.[31] In December 1860 this made Booth a Constitutional Unionist, for a Union recognizing both slavery and the Constitution with its twelve amendments.[32]

Booth's change in political outlook shifted from the prewar rights of the South under the Constitution to secession in his "To Whom It May Concern" letter of November 1864, written in conjunction with a revealing letter to his mother justifying his action of entering a war he had earlier promised to eschew.

Brother Edwin always maintained that Lincoln's November 1864 re-election drove Johnny over the edge, intellectually. After four years of Lincoln's blatantly unconstitutional executive proclamations, including emancipation, Edwin's statement may be true. At least John referred to it obliquely. "I have ever held the South were right," Booth said. "The very nomination of Abraham Lincoln four years ago spoke plainly—war, war upon Southern rights and institutions. His election [in 1860] proved it."[33]

Booth disparaged his earlier stance for Union. "Await an

---

31 Rhodehamel and Taper (eds.), *Writings of John Wilkes Booth*, 60.

32 The pro-slave nature of the original Constitution of 1787 is described in Alfred W. and Ruth G. Blumrosen, *Slave Nation: How Slavery United the Colonies and Sparked the American Revolution* (Naperville, Ills,: Sourcebooks, Inc., 2005) and Paul Finkelman, "Slavery and the Constitutional Convention: Making a Covenant with Death," in Richard Beeman, *et al.* (eds.), *Beyond Confederation: Origins of the Constitution and American National Identity* (Chapel Hill: University of North Carolina Press, 1987), 188-225, and Finkelman, "Garrison's Constitution: The Covenant of Death and How It Was Made," *Prologue: The Magazine of the National Archives*, 32 (2000), 230-45.

33 Edwin's assertion is from Edwin Booth to Nahum Capen, July 28th, 1881, in Stern, *Man Who Killed Lincoln*, 396-97. Booth's statement is from Rhodehamel and Taper (eds.), *Writings of John Wilkes Booth*, 124.

overt act," he spat. "Yes, until you are bound and plundered. What folly, the South were wise [to secede in 1860]." Booth further lamented that "[f]or four years I have waited, hoped and prayed, for the dark clouds to break, and for the restoration of our former sunshine, to wait longer would be a crime." Booth now believed that "[a]ll hope for peace is dead, my prayers have proved as idle as my hopes. God's will be done. I go to see and share the bitter end."[34]

Booth then made what, for him, were two major points. "This country was formed for the *white* not for the black man." Booth said that he looked "upon African slavery from the same stand-point held by those noble framers of our Constitution" as "one of the greatest blessings (both for themselves and for us) that God ever bestowed upon a favored nation."

But the "South *are not, nor have they been fighting* for the continuance of slavery. [T]he first battle of Bull Run did away with that idea," Booth postulated. "Their causes *since* for *war* have been as *noble*, and *greater far than those that* urged our *fathers on*." Booth now saw the Confederates "as a noble band of patriotic heroes" much like the gallant Spartan 300 who stood at Thermopylae. Whatever fault the cause of slavery had it has been erased by Northern "*cruelty and injustice*," which had made any Southern "wrong become the right."[35]

Booth then made his second point. "I have, also, studied hard to discover upon what grounds, the rights of a state to secede have been denied, when the very name (United States) and our Declaration of Independence, *both* provide for secession."[36] But,

---

34 Rhodehamel and Taper (eds.), *Writings of John Wilkes Booth*, 124.

35 *Ibid.*, 125. On Union atrocities in the South, see Walter Brian Cisco, *War Crimes against Southern Civilians* (Gretna, La.: Pelican publishing Company, 2013).

36 Like the seceded states three years earlier, Booth had shifted his political stance from the slavery protections of the Constitution of 1787 to his second choice, the more radical concept of states rights and secession, copied directly from the Declaration of Independence. See Kent Masterson Brown, "Secession: A Constitutional Remedy for the Breach of the Organic Law,"

as usual, Booth did not have the time to go into this in depth, as "I write in haste."[37]

In conclusion, Booth said "I love justice more than I do a country that disowns it. . . . Four years ago I would have given a thousand lives to see her remain (as I had always known her) powerful and unbroken." But now, Booth pledged, "My love (as things stand today) is for the South alone. . . . I go penniless to her side. They say she has found *that* 'last ditch' [in] which the North have . . . been endeavoring to force her," Booth went on. "Should I reach her in safety, . . . I will proudly beg permission to triumph or die in the same 'ditch' by her side."[38]

Booth signed his missive: "*A Confederate doing duty upon his own responsibility.*" To find out what he mean by that, one needs to look at another letter he wrote to his mother about the same time. Booth had promised her not to get involved in the war as it began, but came to regret his vow. "I have always endeavored to be a good and dutiful son," Booth explained, "and would wish to die sooner than give you pain. But dearest Mother, though I owe you all, *there* is another duty. A noble duty for the sake of liberty and humanity due to my Country. . . ."

Booth admitted that he had had a good life in the North, but felt himself constrained, as if he were a slave. "Not daring to express my thoughts or sentiments, even in my own home," Booth related how he was "[c]onstantly hearing every principle, dear to my heart, denounced as treasonable" primarily by

---

North & South, 3 (August 2000), 12-21. The shift of the American South from colony to independence was unique among slaveholding regimes in the New World, seceding as an economic colony of the powerful Great Britain to becoming an economic colony of the weak American North, to developing its own slaveholding rationale in the slavery as a positive good argument (which Booth obviously bought entire [Rhodehamel and Taper (eds.), *Writings of John Wilkes Booth*, 62-63, 125]), to secession from the United States and full independence (which Booth bought, too [*ibid.*, 124-27]) is detailed in Eugene D. Genovese, *The World the Slaveholders Made*, 99-102.

37 Rhodehamel and Taper (eds.), *Writings of John Wilkes Booth*, 125-26.
38 *Ibid.*, 126-27.

his brother Edwin, who compounded everything by just having voted for Lincoln.

"I have cursed my wil[l]ful idleness, [a]nd begun to deem myself a coward," Booth continued, "and to despise my own existence. For four years I have borne it mostly for your sake, [a]nd for you alone, have I also struggled to fight off this desire to be gone...." Then Booth came to the point. "But I cannot longer resist the inclination to go and share the sufferings of my brave countrymen, holding an unequal strife (for every right human & divine) against the most ruthless enemy the world has known."

Booth said, "I feel I *owe the cause I love*, the cause of the South.... So then, *dearest* mother," he ended, "*forgive* and pray for me. I feel I am right in the justness of my cause."[39] The momma's boy had just cut his apron strings at age twenty-six and gone off to war. Booth's secession was total—from country and family.

Booth's final shift in political beliefs from secession to tyrannicide occurred in his "To My Countrymen" letter written for the editors of the *National Intelligencer* newspaper, dated April 14, 1865. Unfortunately there is a real problem with this document. The original does not exist. Booth gave it to his thespian friend, John Matthews, when they casually met on Pennsylvania Avenue the morning of the assassination. Matthews agreed to hand it over to Editor John Coyle, a well-known Southern sympathizer, the next day.[40]

Matthews had no idea what Booth was planning and never read the letter. Indeed it remained conveniently forgotten in this coat pocket until he heard that Booth had assassinated Lincoln. Matthews quickly pulled the letter from his coat, broke open the envelope and read Booth's justification of tyrannicide. Panic-

---

39 *Ibid.*, 130-31.
40 *Ibid.*, 147-53 and footnotes.

stricken that he would be seen as a co-conspirator, he threw the letter into a stove fire to hide the evidence.

Arrested as a friend of Booth, Matthews broke under pressure and admitted he had seen the letter. Federal prosecutors put him on the stand during the trial of Booth co-conspirator John Surratt in 1867 and asked Matthews what the letter said. Matthews really had no idea, but as any good actor would and could, he reconstructed a version of what Booth wrote, relying on his ability to read and memorize passages in plays on short notice. In theater parlance, Matthews "winged it."

The result was two dozen-odd lines of what Booth probably wrote and a lot of borrowed extracts that increased the letter's size from one to three to ten pages (depending on whom Matthews was talking to and when) from Booth's 1860 Philadelphia speech, which by then was widely disseminated in the public. Historians have puzzled over the real or supposed contents of Booth's letter ever since, some saying it never existed, others sure that it did exist, and everyone disputing what it said.

Whatever it was, Matthews' version of the letter to the editors of the *National Intelligencer* was not what Booth really wrote by any stretch of the imagination. But Matthews' twenty-four original lines seem typically Boothian in content, and make up the introduction and conclusion of the document. According to Matthews, Booth began by saying, "[f]or years I have devoted my time, my energies, and every dollar I possessed to the furtherance of an object." Here he was referring to his failed attempts to capture President Lincoln and hie him South for trial or exchange for Southern independence. "I have been baffled and disappointed," Booth groused.

"The hour has come when I must change my plan," he continued.[41] "Many, I know—the vulgar herd—will blame me for

---
41 See John C. Fazio, *Decapitating the Union: Jefferson Davis, Judah Benjamin and the plot*

what I am about to do, but posterity, I am sure, will justify me." Booth, of course, was referring to his assassination of Lincoln, whose election in 1860 had forced Civil War upon the American people—at least in Booth's way of thinking.[42]

"I have ever held that the South were right," Booth asserted. But "[i]f the South is to be aided, it must be done *quickly*. It may already be *too late*," Booth lamented, referring to the fall of Richmond and the surrender of the Army of Northern Virginia at Appomattox. Booth then reminded his readers that when "Caesar had conquered the enemies of Rome and the power that was his menaced the liberties of the people, Brutus arose and slew him. . . . It was the *spirit and ambition* of Caesar that Brutus struck at."

Of course it does not take much imagination even for the modern reader to replace "Caesar" with "Lincoln" and "Brutus" with "Booth."[43] Then Booth quoted directly from Shakespeare's *Julius Caesar*: "Oh that we could come by Caesar's spirit,/ and

---

to Assassinate Lincoln (Jefferson, N.C.: McFarland, 2015), 127-39, who give 26 reasons why the capture of Lincoln never was contemplated as a reality. One is reminded of World War I French Premier Georges Clemenceau's response to President Woodrow Wilson's Fourteen Points: "Quatorze? Le bon Dieu n'a que dix," in William Ralph Inge, *The End of an Age, and Other Essays* (London: Putnam, 1948), 139. Fazio's thesis is denied by Booth, himself, twice, in his letter to the editor of the National Intelligencer, John Coyle, a noted Southern sympathizer, before the Lincoln assassination, which could be considered hearsay, as his friend, actor John McCullough tried to reconstruct the letter after he had burned it, and first-hand in his diary after the deed ("For six months we worked to capture. But our cause being almost lost, something decisive & great must be done"). Rhodehamel and Taper, *Writings of John Wilkes Booth*, 147, 154. The importance and relevance of capturing Lincoln is explained in David W. Gaddy, "Under a Southern Rose: Of a Time When 'CIA' Meant 'Southern Intelligence Activity'," [8], unpublished paper in hands of the author, thanks to Mr. Gaddy.

42 More modern interpretations of Lincoln's forced war between the states include James Ostrowski, "Was the Union Army's Invasion of the Southern States a Legal Act?: An analysis of President Lincoln's Legal Arguments against Secession," in David Gordon, (ed.), *Secession, State & Liberty* (New Brunswick, N.J.: Transaction Publishes, 19980, 155-90; Garrison, *Lincoln's Little War*; Thomas J. DiLorenzo, *The Real Lincoln: A New Look at Abraham Lincoln, His Agenda, and an Unnecessary War* (Roseville, Ca.: Prima Publishing, 2002), 119-21, 259; and William L. Richter, "'Deliberately and Personally Conceived'": Did Abraham Lincoln and the Republicans Intentionally Cause the Civil War?" *infra*, 28-65.

43 The theme of Booth as Brutus is popular in non-fiction (Michael Kauffman, *American Brutus: John Wilkes Booth and the Lincoln Assassination* [New York: Random House, 2004]); and fiction (Diana L. Rubino, *A Necessary End* [Farmington, Mo.: Solstice Publishing, 2014]).

not dismember Caesar!/ But, alas!/ Caesar must bleed for it." Booth closed asserting that he and his co-conspirators were noble "[m]en who love our country better than gold or life." He generously signed the letter with the names of all his cohorts, legally locking them into the conspiracy for all time and, under the law of the day, making them unable to testify against each other in court.[44]

If historians do not know what Booth really wrote in his final political testament, is there a way to approximate it better than Matthews did? Possibly.[45] By examining Booth's statements to his pro-Union family, particularly as recorded by his sister, Asia Booth Clarke, such an understanding might be had.

In several conversations with brother Johnny, Asia remarked how he admitted to being a drug runner, conveying quinine to Southern army purchasers, a drug without which armies on both sides would have been immobilized. Often strange men would come to her house and ask for the "Doctor." "I now knew that my hero was a spy, a blockade-runner, a rebel!" Asia lamented. "I knew he was today what he had been from childhood, an ardent lover of the South and her policy, an upholder of Southern principles."[46]

Another time, Asia remarked how Johnny delighted in singing a parody, each verse ending with a rhyme to a year and then the final line ringing out: "In 1865, when Lincoln shall be king!" Booth firmly believed that the 1860 votes had been manipulated to seat Lincoln as president—"a sectional candidate" Booth dismissed him. He also laughed at how Lincoln had to

---

[44] Rhodehamel and Taper (eds.), *Writings of John Wilkes Booth*, 147, 149-50. Kauffman, *American Brutus*, 172-73, 185, 359-60, explains how Booth worked to extend conspiracy law to every one he could, making it impossible for them to testify against him and each other under the testimony in court rules of the time.

[45] See Richter, *Sic Semper Tyrannis*, 175-83, for such an effort.

[46] Alford (ed.), *John Wilkes Booth: A Sister's Memoir by Asia Booth Clarke*, 82-83.

sneak through Maryland in disguise to claim his seat for the first inauguration.

Booth debased Lincoln, grumbling at his "appearance, his pedigree, his coarse low jokes and anecdotes, his vulgar smiles, and his policy," which Booth condemned as "a disgrace to the seat he holds." Booth asserted, "Other brains rule the country. He is made the tool of the North, to crush out, or try to crush out slavery, by robbery, rapine, slaughter and bought armies."

Then, Booth got to the point. "He is Bonaparte in one great move, that is, by overturning this blind Republic and making himself a king. This man's reelection [in 1864] will be a reign!" Booth thundered. "His kin and friends are in every place of office already."[47]

Actually, despite his often-provocative rhetoric, Booth was not much of a Radical. He was not so much a revolutionary as a conservator. Booth believed in the Declaration of Independence, as it was originally understood in 1776; an assertion, in the words of black historian and magazine editor Lerone Bennett, Jr., that "all [*white*] men are created equal."[48]

Contrary to Booth, Lincoln was the real radical. He wanted the Declaration and, through it the Constitution, changed to its modern interpretation, that "*all* men are created equal," a concept the Railsplitter neatly defined in his 1863 Gettysburg Address, as "a new birth of freedom."[49]

Unlike Lincoln, Booth also stood for the Constitution of 1787, as modified to the Twelfth Amendment, or as anti-Lincoln Democrats from the congressional election of 1862 onward liked to put it, "the Union as it was, the Constitution as it is,

---

47 *Ibid.*, 88.
48 Lerone Bennett, Jr., *Forced into Glory: Abraham Lincoln's White Dream* (Chicago: Johnson Publishing Co., 2000), 82-83 (all white men created equal), 187, 303, 312.
49 Garry Wills, *Gettysburg: The Words that Remade America* (New York: Simon & Schuster, 1992), 121-47.

the Niggers where they are!" This meant the Federal government ought to enforce the Fugitive Slave Law of 1850 (through Article 4, Section 2, Clause 3) and a restrictive role of a Congress limited to its seventeen or so specific powers (Article 1, Section 8) except in the case of slavery's extraterritorial aspects. All else was reserved to the states and/or the people (Amendments Nine and Ten of the Bill of Rights). Lincoln, on the other hand, through the 1860 Republican Platform, envisioned an expanded role for the Federal government in a multitude of areas (tariffs, internal improvements, a national banking system, and the expulsion of former slaves from the United States), mimicking Henry Clay's 1824 American System.[50]

What made Booth appear as the prime radical of his day was his method of political protest, assassination, and the seemingly harsh Reconstruction of the nation that followed.[51] In this act of passion, Booth brought together the two pathways of England's Glorious Revolution of 1688—constitutional government and tyrannicide, something Booth's own grandfather had joined and enshrined when he named one of his sons after the man who epitomized both aspects, Algernon Sydney Booth.[52]

---

50 This is the historically inclined thesis of DiLorenzo, *The Real Lincoln*, 1-9. For a more current politically attuned version, see Thomas J. DiLorenzo, *Lincoln Unmasked: What You're Not Supposed to Know about Dishonest Abe* (New York: Three Rivers Press, 2006), 11-19. For Henry Clay's original American System, see Glyndon G. Van Deusen, *The Jacksonian Era, 1828-1848* (New York: Harper & Row, Publishers, 1959), 51.

51 For ideas as to what a Lincolnian Reconstruction *might* have entailed or actually *did* entail, depending on one's viewpoint (as opposed to what Congress actually imposed on the South), see William Hesseltine, *Lincoln's Plan of Reconstruction* (Tuscaloosa: Confederate Publishing Co., 1960); and Harold Hyman, *Lincoln's Reconstruction: Neither Failure of Vision Nor Vision of Failure* (Ft. Wayne, Ind.: Louis A. Warren Lincoln Library and Museum, 1980). The limitations of Republican policy as to what ought to have happened to freed slaves after the war is explored in C. Vann Woodward, "Seeds of Failure in Radical Race Policy" in Harold Hyman (ed.), *New Frontiers of the American Reconstruction* (Urbana: University of Illinois Press, 1966), 124-47. A general essay on the nature of Reconstruction is William L. Richter, "Introduction: The Historians and Reconstruction," *The ABC-Clio Companion to American Reconstruction, 1862-1865* (Santa Barbara, Calif.: ABC-Clio, 1896), xix-lv.

52 The best short treatment of Algernon Sidney (who was executed by Charles II for his role in justifying the execution of Charles I) is Caroline Robbins, "Algernon Sidney's *Discourses Concerning Government*: Textbook of Revolution," *William and Mary Quarterly*, Series 3, 4

Booth's solution to the whole debate was the same as his uncle's namesake, "pulling down the Colossus," or committing what twentieth century British poet and social commentator, W. H. Auden, once defined as a "necessary murder."[53] The elimination the President, who brought secession and war about through his duplicitous speeches and executive proclamations devoid of congressional input, was the only truly radical contribution he made.[54]

In this Booth acted in his own mind not as a murderer but as a soldier who shot down the enemy commander-in-chief in the final military special operation of the war.[55] He fully understood the fine distinction made by the French philosopher Voltaire: "Killing a man is murder *unless* you do it to the sound of trumpets." Booth heard the trumpets. His tragedy is that Americans (then and now) remain tone deaf to his music.

As his schoolmates had warned, Booth merely brought the Colossus down upon himself. Paralyzed from a shot through his neck at Garrett's farm in Virginia twelve days after assassinating Lincoln, a dying Booth gasped to his pursuers, "Tell mother I died for my country." What he meant to say, had he but the strength to utter the words, was what he told his school chums

---

(1947), 267-96; see also, Alan Craig Houston, *Algernon Sidney and the Republican Heritage in England and America*. (Princeton: Princeton University Press, 1991), and Jonathan Scott, *Algernon Sidney and the English Republic, 1623-1677* (Cambridge: Cambridge University Press, 1988) and his *Algernon Sidney and the Restoration Crisis, 1677-1683* (Cambridge: Cambridge University Press, 1991). In his attack on John Marshall and his aggrandizement of power through the U.S. Supreme Court after the War of 1812, Virginia Justice Spencer Roane used the pseudonym "Algernon Sydney" to make his point. See Forrest McDonald, *States' Rights and the Union: Imperium in Imperio, 1776-1876* (Lawrence: The University Press of Kansas, 2000), 78.

53 Auden, "Spain," pamphlet privately published (1939).

54 See William L. Richter, *The Assassinator: The Trial and Hanging of John Wilkes Booth* (Tucson, Az.: Wheatmark, 2015), 89-163. For a different approach, see Don Thomas, *The Reason Lincoln Had to Die* (Chesterfield, Va.: Pumphouse Publishers, 2013).

55 William Hanchett, "Lincoln's Assassination as a Military Necessity," unpublished ms., copy in Lincoln Folder, Drawer #9, William A. Tidwell papers, James O Hall Research Center, Surtratt Society, Clinton Md.; Gaddy, "Under a Southern Rose," [8], unpublished paper in hands of the author, thanks to Mr. Gaddy.

a decade before at St. Timothy's Academy: "I should die with the satisfaction of knowing I had done something never before accomplished by any other man, and something no other man would do."

II.

"Deliberately and Personally Conceived"

Did Abraham Lincoln and the Republicans Intentionally Cause the Civil War?

The rationale of the Secession Movement and the ensuing War for Southern Independence was never put forth more eloquently than in a suggested resolution by Mildred "Miz Milly" Rutherford, the historian of the United Daughters of the Confederacy, at the association's joint reunion with the United Confederate Veterans, Sons of Confederate Veterans, Confederated Southern Memorial Association, and "Other Organizations" at Richmond, Virginia, in 1922:

> "The War Between the States was deliberately and personally conceived and its inauguration made by Abraham Lincoln, and he was personally responsible for forcing the war upon the South." [56]

Miz Millie brought down the house, as Rebel yells, cheers,

---

56   Merrill D. Peterson, *Lincoln in American Memory* (Oxford University Press, 1994), 251, quoting the *Confederate Veteran*, 30 (1922), 286-86. For the key role of women like Miz Millie in refusing to let bygones be bygones after the war, see Caroline E. Janney, "Hell Hath No Fury," *The Civil War Monitor*, 3 (Fall 2013), 58-67, especially 66-67 for Miz Millie. See also, John McKee Barr, *Loathing Lincoln: An American Tradition from the Civil War to the Present* (Baton Rouge: Louisiana State University Press, 2014), 9, 131, 134, 139-41, 148,

and applause erupted from the adoring crowd before the dais. Her resolution was quickly adopted by acclamation. Nowadays, we chuckle and scoff at such presentments, but the question remains—is it possible that she was right?

John Wilkes Booth thought so.[57] He called Secession, much as did out-going President James Buchanan,[58] "a fire lighted and fanned by Northern fanaticism," and said that Lincoln's nomination as the Republican presidential candidate was but a declaration of "war, war upon Southern institutions. His election proved it." Unlike Booth, however, modern Americans, of course, will not believe Miz Millie's assertion as it goes against currently accepted history. But we would do well to remember the old adage: "history is written by those who have hanged the heroes."[59]

To begin with, one must realize what was at stake in 1860— that abolition of slavery in the existing states was *not* the issue. In fact, Lincoln and the Republicans said that they were willing to guarantee slavery where it existed by a new irrevocable constitutional amendment.

Indeed, the only real way slavery could be destroyed in the states was by a constitutional amendment, which was practically impossible to achieve. This is because it takes three-fourths of the states to amend the Constitution, and the Slave South, being nearly half of the states, thus had a veritable veto. But, in agreeing to maintain slavery in the states where it existed, Lincoln and the Republicans never consented *not* to constrict slavery where it was or hamper the spread of slavery, elsewhere.[60]

---

57 John Rodehamel and Louise Taper, *"Right ot Wrong, God Judge Me": The Wrtitings of John Wilkes Booth* (Urbana: University of Illinois Press, 1997), 59, 124.

58 Buchanan's 1860 Annual Message, paraphrased in Allan Nevins, *The Emergence of Lincoln: Prologue to Civil War, 1859-1861* (2 vols., New York: Charles Scribner's Sons, 1950), II, 352-53.

59 Robert the Bruce in the voice-over introduction to the movie *Braveheart* (1995).

60 Bestor, "State Sovereignty and Slavery, 122-27.

Before the creation of the Republican Party in 1854, as historian David Brion Davis points out, no other political party had really seriously challenged the westward expansion of slavery.[61] By 1860, however, fortified by cobbling together the diverse supporters of what Southern apologist George Fitzugh called the pre-Civil War "infidel Isms of the North," Republicans pledged no more "milk and water" policy against slavery.[62] Everyone soon realized what Republican policy, despite all of its duplicitous protect slavery promises, meant for the future of the South and its domestic institutions. The Republicans would attack slavery as soon as Lincoln came into power.[63]

As contemporaries, North and South perceived, the Republican program against slavery, characterized by Charles Sumner, master orator and U.S. senator from Massachusetts, as making Freedom National and Slavery Sectional,[64] was comprised of two elements: The Cordon of Freedom, and Military Emancipation. The Cordon of Freedom was an old anti-slavery belief that if bondage could be isolated to the existing slave states with no hope for expansion into the West or the Caribbean, it would wither away in time and die out. Hence, Lincoln's promise to leave slavery intact where it was in the states was really a misleading statement in light of the Cordon of Freedom. Its corollary, Military Emancipation, was the notion that should the

---

61 David Brion Davis, "American Slavery and the American Revolution," in his *From Homicide to Slavery: Studies in American Culture* (New York: Oxford University Press, 1986), 299.

62 Kevin Phillips, *The Cousins' Wars: Religion, Politics, and the Triumph of Anglo-America* (New York: Basic Books, 1999), 353-62 (especially 357-58 and 362), and 383 (Fitzhugh quote).

63 Don Fehrenbacher with Ward M. McAfee, *Slaveholding Republic: An Account of the United States Government's Relations to Slavery* (New York: Oxford University Press, 2001), 295-96.

64 James Oakes, *Freedom National: The Destruction of Slavery in the United States, 1861-1865* (New York: Norton, 2013), 32. The term "Freedom National" may actually have originated with or been popularized by Republican Governor of Indiana, Oliver P. Morton. See Oakes, *The Scorpions' Sting: Anti-Slavery and the Coming of the Civil War* (New York: Norton, 2014), 28. A good review and synopsis of both volumes is in Andrew Delbanco, "The Civil War Convulsion," *The New York Review of Books*, LII (March 19, 2015), 30-33.

South secede it would lose all the slavery protections guaranteed in the Constitution, and the advancing, all-conquering, Federal armies could abolish slavery outright.

If slavery in the states was not the real issue, what was? It was more than Union. It was the *extraterritorial implications* of slavery as an institution, written into the Constitution of 1787.[65] This was revealed in the two sectional issues that pestered the nation between the War with Mexico and the Civil War, the operations of the fugitive slave law, and slavery extension into the western territories of the United States.

What the South held, basically, was that slaveholding states were justified in controlling the internal policies of non-slaveholding states whenever those policies adversely affected, even indirectly, the institution of slavery. This was the essence of extraterritoriality. Found in Article IV, Section 2, Clause 3, the fugitive clause was critical to the Southern viewpoint on the extraterritoriality of slavery. It read:

> No Person held to Service or Labour in one State, under the laws thereof, escaping into another [State] shall, in Consequence of any Law or Regulation therein, be discharged from such Service or Labour, but shall be deliv-

---

[65] Contrary to the editor's argument in Don E. Fehrenbacher, *The Slaveholding Republic: An Account of the United States Government's Relations to Slavery* (New York: Oxford University Press, 2001), that the U.S. Constitution was neither a pro or anti-slavery document, anti-slavery Northerners came to fear that the Constitution was so tainted in favor of slavery that it might have to be replaced with a new document, until Republicans decided it was a good document that merely need to be purged of its pro-slavery sentiments. This was accomplished by William H. Whiting of the Adjutant General's Department in his 1862 treatise, *War Powers of the President*, later expanded into *War Powers under the Constitution of the United States*. See Michael Les Benedict, *Preserving the Constitution: Essays on Politics and the Constitution in the Reconstruction Era* (Fordham University Press, May 2006). See also, Harold M. Hyman, *A More Perfect Union: The Impact of the Civil War and Reconstruction on the Constitution* (Boston: Houghton Mifflin, 1975), 99-140; and Paul C. Nagel, *One Nation Indivisible: The Union in American Thought, 1776-1861* (New York: Oxford University Press, 1964). Also of interest are Richard Morris, *The Forging of the Union, 1781-1789* (Cambridge: Harper & Row, 1987), Donald L. Robinson, *Slavery in the Structure of American Politics, 1765-1821* (New York: Harcourt, Brace, Jovanovich, 1971); and Larry Gara, "Slavery and the Slave Power: A Crucial Distinction," *Civil War History*, 15 (1969), 5-18.

ered up on Claim of the Party to whom such Service or Labour may be due.[66]

This clause does not refer to criminal extradition, which is treated in Article IV, Section 2, Clause 2, in which the governor of a state has the right under state law to deny returning a person charged with "Treason, Felony or other Crime" to the state where the alleged crime was committed.[67]

The guaranteed fugitive return in Clause 3, called recaption, referred to slaves (those "held to Service or Labour" in the Constitution's more delicate language) to whom bondage clung no matter where in the Union they might flee or be taken by their owner. The slave law of any slave state was to be enforced by the federal government in any other jurisdiction in the Union, even if it were a free state or a free territory.

Not so open and shut, was the concept that extraterritoriality was to play in the premier pre-Civil War issue—the expansion of slavery into the western territories, particularly after the American victory in the War with Mexico. It was here that the Southern view of extraterritoriality revealed itself as a blatant tenet of domestic political power to promote the creation of new slave states through something called the non-exclusion doctrine.[68]

As the Slave South was aware, the ability of slaveholding Americans to move west with their slaves into the territories and to hold them and exploit their labor there was an extraterritorial right. They would be living beyond their state of origin, expect-

---

66 Bestor, "State Sovereignty and Slavery, 127-30.

67 *Annot. Constit.* (http://www.eco.freedom.org/ac92/ac92pgix.shtml), 878-881. Standards of extradition are much more regularized nowadays. See Edwin Meese III, *et al.* (eds.), *The Heritage Guide to the Constitution* (Washington, D.C.: Regnery, 2005), 273-75.

68 Bestor, "State Sovereignty and Slavery," 147-62, for a discussion of slavery in the territories.

ing protection of their slave property, as if they were still at home in the South. The problem arose because territorial government was not really mentioned in the Constitution. Only state and federal government were. But the Union had almost always had three elements, state, federal, and territorial.

Most Americans, North or South, were cognizant of the fact that the real question was which entity (state, federal or territorial) was to exercise control over domestic social policy, the so-called police power, involving the regulation of behavior and enforcement of order within its boundaries for the betterment of health, safety, general welfare, and morals of the population at large, which included local slave codes.[69] The U.S. Constitution left this up to the states under the Tenth Amendment, but no real constitutionally defined government existed in the territories, which were not co-equal to the states.[70]

The question of free or pro-slave states had not been much of a problem prior to the War with Mexico, as free and slave states had been admitted into the Union in pairs, which kept a North-South equilibrium in the U.S. Senate. True, there had been a flare-up in 1820, when the admission of Missouri as a slave state threatened to tilt the balance toward the South, but

---

69 Police power was a term first coined by Chief Justice Taney in another context back in 1827 (as an attorney practicing before the Sup. Ct.), see Charles Warren, *The Supreme Court in United States History, 1789-1918* (2 vols., Boston: Little, Brown & Co., 1922), I, 695 n.2. A good listing of the state police powers is in Forrest McDonald, *States' Rights and the Union: Imperium in Imperio, 1776-1876* (Lawrence: University of Kansas Press, 2000), 223.

70 This is where the South differed from Lincoln and Northern Democrat and Lincoln rival in Illinois, U.S. Senator Stephen A. Douglas. Lincoln backed Squatter Sovereignty, the notion of former Democratic presidential candidate Lewis Cass that the slavery question in a territory could be decided by the territorial legislature. Lincoln forced Douglas to abandon his Popular Sovereignty, the Southern Non-exclusion Doctrine, in the Lincoln-Douglas Debates of 1858, with the so-called Freeport Doctrine. In this, Douglas stated that a territorial legislature could deny slavery legal protection and thus its efficacy at any time before it became a state. This won Douglas the U.S. Senate seat from Illinois in 1858 but cost Douglas Southern support for the presidency in 1860 and guaranteed Lincoln's nomination by the Republicans as a moderate anti-slavery man. See Roy Basler (ed.), *The Collected Works of Abraham Lincoln* (9 vols., New Brunswick: Rutgers University Press, 1953), III, 43 (Freeport Question), 51-52 (Freeport Doctrine).

this had been dampened when Massachusetts allowed its northern-most county to be admitted as the free and separate state of Maine.

Hereafter, according to this so-called Missouri Compromise, any new territories in the Louisiana Purchase (1803) would be free states if they were incorporated north of the line 36°30', the southern boundary of Missouri. This meant that slavery expansion in the West would be restricted to the territories of Arkansas and the Indian Nations (essentially modern Oklahoma) between 1820 and 1845.[71]

But the Annexation of Texas (1845) and War with Mexico (1846-48) opened up a whole lot of territory below the Missouri Compromise line and south of the Louisiana Purchase. The North, in effect, had fought a war to open up a vast area in the Mexican Cession of the American Southwest to be potential slave states, under the terms of the Missouri Compromise.

Northern congressmen had cried foul even before the Mexican War started. They introduced the Wilmot Proviso in 1846, as the war began, proposing that any territorial concession from Mexico would be without slavery. The South demurred and, although the Wilmot Proviso passed the Yankee-dominated U.S. House of Representatives, Southern senators blocked it in the equally divided U.S. Senate,[72] holding out for the non-exclusion of slavery in all territories as an extraterritorial right.

---

71 For the Missouri Compromise, see Glover Moore, *The Missouri Controversy, 1819-1821* (Lexington: University of Kentucky Press, 1966); Richard Holbrook Brown, *The Missouri Compromise: Political Statesmanship or Unwise Evasion?* (Boston: Heath, 1964); Tristram Potter Coffin, *The Missouri Compromise* (Boston: Little Brown, 1947); Frank H. Hodder, "Side Lights on the Missouri Compromises," in American Historical Association, Reports (1909), pp. 151-161. On an congressionally-agreed-upon exception to the 36°30' rule concerning the Platte Region in northwestern Missouri, see H. Jason Combs, "The South's Slave Culture Transplanted to the Western Frontier," *The Professional Geographer: Forum and Journal of the Association of American Geographers*, 56 (2004), 361-71.

72 Both Florida and Texas had been admitted in before the Mexican War, while Iowa and Wisconsin came in during the War with Mexico, giving the South a temporary majority in the Senate. See Paul Finkelman, "Dred Scott, Slavery, and the Politics of Law," *Hamline Law Review*, 20 (1996), 1-42, at 34n119. Until 1858, however, the South was usually assisted in

But it was obvious that Congress somehow would have to administer the territories in the West before they achieved statehood, and the Constitution allowed for such governance,[73] without defining what territories were or what "needful rules and regulations" like the police powers or a slave code might be demanded there.

The Slave South argued that the exercise of this police power was the prerogative of a sovereign. The citizens of a territory lacked complete sovereignty because they shared rule with the federal government under the provisions of the Northwest Ordinance or the Land Ordinance of 1787, which described the steps by which a territory became a state.[74] Hence, without complete sovereignty, the citizens of a territory could *not* vote on slavery *before* the territory became a state, a process known as Squatter Sovereignty in the Election of 1848, which was favored by most Northerners, including Abraham Lincoln.[75]

Congress, without an outright delegation by the states of their sovereign power over the territories to the Federal government, had no sovereignty there, either. Indeed, the Tenth Amendment stated that, in a government of delegated powers

---

its control of both houses of Congress by northerners sympathetic to slavery, either morally or politically. See Leonard L. Richards, *The Slave Power: The Free North and Southern Domination, 1780-1860* (Baton Rouge: Louisiana State University Press, 2000).

73   Article IV, Section 3, Clause 2.

74   Ray Allen Billington, "The Historians of the Northwest Ordinance," Illinois State Historical Society, *Journal*, 40 (1947), 347-413; Jack E. Eblen, "The Origins of the United States Colonial System: The Ordinance of 1787," *Wisconsin Magazine of History*, 51 (1968), 294-314; Frederick D. Stone, "The Ordinance of 1787," *Pennsylvania Magazine of History and Biography*, 25 (1938), 167-80; Staughton Lynd, "The Compromise of 1787," *Political Science Quarterly*, 81 (1966), 225-50; Merrill Jensen, "The Creation of the National Domain, 1781-1784," *Mississippi Valley Historical Review*, 26 (1939), 323-42; T.C. Pease, "The Ordinance of 1787," ibid., 25 (1938): 167-80; Frederick D. Williams (ed.), Northwest Ordinance: Essays on Its Formulation, Provisions, and Legacy (Lansing: Michigan State University Press, 1989). See also, Paul Finkelman, "Slavery and the Northwest Ordinance: A Study in Ambiguity," *Journal of the Early Republic*, 6 (1986), 343-70.

75   Michael Burlingame, *Abraham Lincoln: A Life* (2 vols., Baltimore: The Johns Hopkins University Press, 2008), I, 385. Neither Lincoln nor his biographer, Burlingame, understand this concept.

as existed under the Constitution, the local police powers were reserved only to *sovereign states* admitted into the Union.

But it was obvious that each individual state could not enforce its own concept of police powers in any or all territories. That would create rank confusion. The solution was for the states to allow the federal government to function as their agent. The federal government would act on the slavery question in the territories not as the government of the *United* States but as the trustee of the *States* united.

That is to say, the federal government, in the matter of slavery in the territories alone, would act as a mere deputy, a representative to give every state's laws an extraterritorial effect.

The Constitution, of course, specifically said which laws had an extraterritorial character. The *only* state laws that had extraterritorial effect were the laws pertaining to slavery through the fugitive recaption clause of the Constitution, Article IV, Section 2, Clause 3.[76] There was no discretion or deliberation allowed here. The federal government was to administrate, not legislate.

This so-called non-exclusion doctrine (*i.e.*, no prior exclusion of slavery in any western territories before statehood—also known as the Alabama Platform in the Election of 1848, and Popular Sovereignty in both the Election of 1852 and Kansas Nebraska Act of 1854, the latter of which brought Whig politician Abraham Lincoln back into politics as a Republican) paid off big in 1857 in the case of Scott v. Sanford.[77]

---

76 Bestor, "State Sovereignty and Slavery," 147-62, for a discussion of exraterritoriality. Edward E. Baptist, *The Half Has Never Been Told: Slavery and the Making of American Capitalism* (New York: Basic Books, 2014), 329-32, relies on a John C. Calhoun speech in the Senate in February 1847, which relied on the Fifth Amendment to the Constitution. Bestor has the better explanation here, reling on Art. IV, Sec. 2 of the unamended Constitution.

77 Dred Scott v. John F.A. Sanford, *et al.*, 19 Howard at 393. See Bestor, "State Sovereignty and Slavery," 167-72; Paul Finkelman, "What Did the Dred Scott Case Really Decide?" *Reviews in American History*, 7 (1979), 368-74. See also, Robert M.Cover, *Justice Accused: Antislavery and Judicial Process* (New Haven: Yale University Press, 1975); Don E. Fehrenbacher, *The Dred Scott Case: Its Significance in American Law and Politics* (New York: Oxford University Press, 1978); Paul Finkelman, *An Imperfect Union: Slavery, Federalism, and Comity* (Chapel

Dred Scott was a slave in Missouri owned by an army surgeon, Dr. John Emerson, who had legally bought him while serving at Jefferson Barracks below St. Louis. As an army doctor, Emerson changed duty stations frequently. Among others, he went to Ft. Armstrong, at Rock Island, Illinois, a free territory under the Northwest Ordinance of 1787 and a free state since its admission to the Union in 1818; then to Ft. Snelling (present-day Minneapolis), Minnesota, a free territory under the 1820 Missouri Compromise.

To each post, Emerson took his slave, Dred Scott, with him. Eventually, Dr. Emerson returned to St. Louis, where he obligingly died (for the sake of our story) in 1843 at age 40 from the advanced stages of syphilis, passing his property, including Dred Scott, to Mrs. Irene Emerson and their newborn daughter (both of whom, evidently, remained free of the disease).

Mrs. Emerson permitted her brother, John F.A. Sanford,[78] to administer the estate. Sanford regularly hired Dred Scott out to other people, a common practice, particularly in the Border South states like Missouri. Scott even went into disputed Mexican territory before the war, a country that had banned slavery in 1821, as a slave hired out to a U.S. Army officer.

When he returned to St. Louis after the war, Scott asked to buy himself out of slavery. Mrs. Emerson, through Sanford, refused. Scott then sued for his freedom, claiming that he had

---

Hill: University of North Carolina Press, 1981); Vincent C. Hopkins, *Dred Scott's Case* (New York: Fordham University Press, 1951); Harold M. Hyman, and William Wiecek. *Equal Justice under Law: Constitutional Development, 1835-1875* (New York: Harper & Row, 1982); Stanley I. Kutler (ed.), *The Dred Scott Decision: Law or Politics?* (Boston: Houghton Mifflin Co., 1967); E. I. McCormick, "Justice Campbell and the Dred Scott Decision," *Mississippi Valley Historical Review*, 19 (1933), 565-71; Frank H. Hodder, "Some Phases of the Dred Scott Case," *Mississippi Valley Historical Review*, 16 (June 1929), 3-22.

78 Sanford was the principal representative in St. Louis for John Jacob Astor's American Fur Company out of New York City. See Hiram M. Chittenden, *The American Fur Trade of the Far West* (2 vols., Lincoln: University of Nebraska Press, 1986 reprint of 1935 edition), I, 373n5. But he administered the Emerson estate as a citizen from New York.

falsely been enslaved in a free territory and in a free state and in a free country (Mexico).

Scott lost his suit in the local court, but won it in the Missouri district court. Sanford, claiming Scott was a citizen of Missouri and he a citizen of New York (where he had been born), took the case to federal court. By now the lawsuit had become a *cause célèbre* and big name Republican lawyers, like Edward Bates (Lincoln's future attorney general) and Frank Blair, Jr. (his brother, Montgomery, would be Lincoln's postmaster general), volunteered to represent Scott, *pro bono*. Scott lost again in the U.S. circuit court, and appealed the case to the U.S. Supreme Court.

Meanwhile, to thoroughly complicate things, Mrs. Emerson got remarried to a Yankee abolitionist congressman, moved to Massachusetts, and, imbued with love in more aspects than one, saw the error of her prior slaveholding ways, and freed Dred Scott and his family. In reality there was no real case, because Scott would now go free no matter what the U.S. Supreme Court ruled.

But the legal myth of Scott's continued slavery was maintained until the law suit ran its course, with the St. Louis County sheriff administering the hiring and putting the wages Scott earned in a trust to be paid to whichever side won the litigation. The case of Scott v. Sanford was decided in March 1857. At that time, the U.S. Supreme Court had nine members. They were seven Jacksonian Democrats (five of whom were slave holders), one Whig, and one Republican.

Hence, it was no surprise that the court ruled seven to two that Dred Scott was still a slave. But no one could agree as to why. Each judge wrote a separate opinion, so it was the ruling of the Chief Justice, Roger B. Taney of Maryland,[79] concurred

---

79 On Taney, see Charles W. Smith, Jr., *Roger B. Taney: Jacksonian Jurist* (Chapel Hill:

with in part by several other associate judges, which became the accepted majority opinion. A strict interpreter of the Constitution rather than a pro-slave advocate, as modern historians often wrongly assert,[80] Taney was a slaveholder who found slavery distasteful in the long run and emancipated his slaves long before the Civil War, providing for their upkeep.

In the Scott case, Taney said that blacks were not citizens of the state of Missouri and never had been. Hence Scott could not even bring suit in state or federal court. Indeed, Taney noted that even most free states refused to allow Negro citizenship (which at that time was a state matter before the Fourteenth Amendment made citizenship a federal question in 1867).

Taney should have stopped right there and thrown the case out of court. But the Chief Justice and the Slave South had been waiting a long time for this opportunity, and Taney was not going to let it go to waste. A slave's mere residence in, or transit through, a free state or a free territory did not free a slave, Taney went on. This was because Article IV, Section 2, Clause 3 of the U.S. Constitution gave slavery an extraterritorial quality that had to be enforced everywhere in the nation.

Only when a territory gained its complete, undivided sovereignty through becoming a state, could it legislate against slavery within its own boundaries, Taney ruled. Until then, Congress and the federal government were but trustees or temporary caretakers to administer all extraterritorial powers of slavery.

This meant that the Missouri Compromise of no slavery

University of North Carolina Press, 1936); Carl Brent Swisher, *Roger B. Taney* (New York: Macmillan, 1935); H.H. Walker Lewis, *Without Fear or Favor: A Biography of Chief Justice Roger B. Taney* (Boston: Houghton Mifflin, 1965); Paul Finkelman, "Hooted Down the Pages of History?: Reconsidering the Greatness of Chief Justice Taney," *1994 Journal of the Supreme Court History* (1995), 83-102.

80 McPherson, *Battle Cry of Freedom*, 173, referencing Don E. Fehrenbacher, "Roger B. Taney and the Sectional Crisis," *Journal of Southern History*, 43 (1977), 555-66. See also, Finkelman, "Hooted Down the Pages of History,'" 97.

in *some* territories was unconstitutional. So was the Wilmot Proviso of no slavery extension into *any* territories obtained from Mexico. So was squatter sovereignty, because it occurred before the territory gained full sovereignty by becoming a state. But the Alabama Platform of 1848, the non-exclusion doctrine allowing slavery in all territories before statehood, also called popular sovereignty and endorsed by the Kansas-Nebraska Act, was constitutional.

This, then, was the extraterritoriality of slavery promised by the U.S. Constitution—guaranteed fugitive recaption and no prior limits to slavery extension into the territories. Lincoln spoke of extraterritoriality in his House Divided Speech, when he said, "A house divided against itself cannot stand. . . . Either the *opponents* of slavery will arrest the further spread of it," Lincoln maintained, "or its *advocates* will push it forward, till it shall become lawful in *all* states, *old* as well as *new*—*North* as well as *South*."

Actually, what Lincoln really feared more than *Dred Scott*, was a new case on extraterritoriality that was wending its way through the New York court system, Lemmon v. the People of New York. The Lemmon family was moving to Texas in 1852, a common thing in the 1850s, North and South. But the Lemmons were taking their half-dozen slaves with them.

Docking in New York from Virginia, before boarding the Texas-bound ship, the Lemmons' slaves were held in a local jail, standard procedure for transporting slaves over distance. A local Free Man of Color found out and went to New York state courts to obtain a writ of habeas corpus to free the slaves under an 1817 state law that prohibited the transport or importation of slaves into the state under any pretense. The New York courts quickly ruled the Lemmons' slaves to be free.

The Lemmons appealed the case through the state court system, maintaining that their slaves were personal property guaranteed equal treatment throughout the Union by the Fourth Amendment to the Constitution, but losing their case two more times by 1860. The next stop was Federal court system, capped off by a trip to the U.S. Supreme Court, Chief Justice Taney presiding, with the same bench that ruled Dred Scott a slave after all his travels through free jurisdictions. A similar ruling in Lemmon would in effect make slavery legal in all states and territories of the United States, so long as the owner kept citizenship in his home state. Slavery would then be truly national, as Lincoln posited in his House Divided Speech.

Lincoln concluded, "I do not expect the Union to be *dissolved* . . . but I *do* expect it will cease to be divided."[81] So far, however, Lincoln and the Republicans lacked not only the constitutional basis, but the national political power necessary to enact their hoped-for Cordon of Freedom.

Lincoln and the Republicans believed that their inability to impose the Cordon of Freedom legally or constitutionally was because of the existence of what they called the Slave Power Conspiracy,[82] which they believed infected the Federal government at all levels. Between 1789 and 1861, in a nation where free, white males (potential voters) in the Northern states outnumbered Southern whites at least two to one, the South secured

---

81 Basler (ed.), *The Collected Works of Abraham Lincoln*, II, 461-62 (quotes), 464-67. See also, Alexander Gigante, "Slavery and a House Divided," at http://afroamhistory.about.com/library/prm/blhousedivided. httm; Paul Finkelman, "The Nationalization of Slavery: A Counter-factual Approach to the 1860s," *Louisiana Studies*, 14 (Fall 1975), 213-40, Doris Kearns Goodwin, *Team of Rivals : The Political Genius of Abraham Lincoln* (New York: Simon & Schuster Paperbacks, 2005), 199.

82 The name "Slave Power" originated in Massachussetts with Liberty Party Activist, Joshua Leavitt in his publication, the *Emancipatioinist*. Baptist, *Half Has Never Been Told*, 325. Others credit U.S. Senator Thomas Morris of Ohio. See Leonard L. Richards, *The Slave Power: The Free North and Southern Domination, 1780-1860* (Baton Rouge: Louisiana State University Press, 2000), 23. In the control of the Federal government and the Democratic Party, see Michael Todd Landis, *Northern Men with Southern Loyalties: The Democratic Party and the Sectional Crisis* (Ithica: Cornell University Press, 2014).

fully half of all major cabinet and diplomatic appointments, and had 22 extra representatives in the lower house of Congress from counting three-fifths of its slaves. The Old South, more or less, according to this theory, unfairly and disproportionately ran the whole nation.[83]

Not counting numerous clerkships, secretaries, sergeants at arms, and pages in every executive and congressional department of the federal government, which, in that age of difficult and expensive travel, frequently went to local Washingtonians, Marylanders, and Virginians (who generally backed the institution of slavery if they were not slaveholders themselves), individual presidential administrations tended to be very lop-sided in their appointment policies. Fifty-one percent of John Adams' appointments were Southern slave owners. But Thomas Jefferson made 56 percent of his appointments from the Old South, while Andrew Jackson found 57 percent of his appointments among slaveholders.

In the 62 years between 1789 and 1850, slaveholders controlled the presidency for 50 years, and five of these slaveholders (George Washington, Thomas Jefferson, James Madison, James Monroe, and Andrew Jackson) served two consecutive terms. No Northerner was ever reelected to the presidency before the Civil War, regardless of his stance on slavery. The northern-born, pro-slave presidents of the 1850s (Millard Fillmore of New York,

---

[83] In general, see William L. Richter, *Historical Dictionary of the Old South* (Lanham, Md.: Scarecrpw Press, 2013), 10-13. More specific studies include Larry Gara, "Slavery and the Slave Power: A Crucial Distinction," *Civil War History*, 15 (1969), 5-18; Alfred W. and Ruth G. Blumenrosen, *Slave Nation: How Slavery United the Colonies & Sparked the American Revolution* ((Napierville, Ills.: Sourcebooks, Inc., 2005); David Waldstreicher, *Slavery's Constitution from Revolution to Ratification* (New York: Hill & Wang, 2009); Paul Finkelman, *Slavery and the Founders: Race and Liberty in the Age of Jefferson* (Armonk, N.Y.: M.E. Sharpe, 1996); Garry Wills, *"Negro President": Jefferson and the Slave Power* (Boston: Houghton Mifflin Co., 2003); Davis Brion Davis, *The Slave Power Conspiracy and the Paranoid Style* (Baton Rouge: Louisiana State University Press, 1969); Richards, *The Slave Power*. Fehrenbacher and McAfee, *Slaveholding Republic*, ix, see this as an unintended result over time, rather than a "conspiracy" intentionally installed at the brginning of the nation.

Franklin Pierce of New Hampshire, and James Buchanan of Pennsylvania) continued this pro-slavery trend to the Civil War.

Additionally, for 51 of the 62 years, the Speaker of the House was a slaveholder and the longest serving speakers were all Southerners, Henry Clay (Kentucky), Andrew Stevenson (Virginia), and Nathaniel Macon (North Carolina). The chairmen of the powerful House Ways and Means Committee (which determined what legislation reached the floor) were slaveholders for 41 of those 62 years. Eighteen of 31 Supreme Court justices from the same period were from the Old South, as were the two more important chief justices, John Marshall (Virginia) and Roger B. Taney (Maryland).

There is more involved in this political ascendancy than the three-fifths compromise in the Constitution, which guaranteed the Old South 22 extra congressmen in the 1850s, based on the enumeration of slaves in the U.S. census. This Southern dominance was made possible by the support that non-slave holding, Northern congressmen, Democrats after the rise of Jackson, rendered to Southern positions on slavery. These men actually came to the fore during the debates on the Missouri Compromise. It was their votes that made the adjustment of sectional argument over the admission of Missouri as a slave state possible. They were condemned as "unblushing advocates of domestic slavery" by their opponents in the North.

But it took the invective of a Southerner, who distrusted them as much as their Northern critics, to give them the sobriquet by which they would be forever known all the way to the Civil War. John Randolph of Roanoke, Virginia, called them "doughfaces,"[84] Northerners of Southern principle, and he

---

84 The name comes from a children's game in which players disguised themselves by placing pieces of dough on their faces. See Landis, *Northern Men with Southern Loyal*ties, 4.

despised them for being bought off by political patronage and deemed them unreliable for the future.[85]

Master 19th Century politician Martin Van Buren organized these doughfaces, and others of like philosophy, into a paramount part of his new national Democratic Party that made Andrew Jackson and his successors president.

Randolph proved correct in his prediction of their final fecklessness, but it would take the bitter anti-slavery quarrels of the 1850s and the rise of the Republican Party to cause the doughfaces to break their bond with the Old South. Those who had stayed loyal to the Southern wing of the Democratic Party, the old Jacksonians from New York and elsewhere, men who had traditionally delivered 15-25 votes in Congress to protect Southern rights in slaves and territorial expansion, ultimately changed their views on slavery and either became strong anti-slavery men or lost election to Republicans or Free Soil independents. Thus, by 1860, the Old South could still block legislation, but it could no longer advance its program defending the extraterritoriality of slavery in the territories because of the loss of its Northern allies.[86]

The South felt the loss of its political power in Congress as early as 1859, when the Whig Representative from Baltimore's Fourth Congressional District, Henry Winter Davis, switched sides to vote Republican William Pennington in as speaker of the house, and was promptly censured by the Maryland State

---

[85] On Randolph, see Russell Kirk, *John Randolph of Roanoke: A Study in American Politics* (Indianapolis: Liberty Press, 1978).

[86] Ironically, with the end of slavery at the termination of the Civil War, and the counting of the African Americans as full persons, the Northern victory actually increased the native-born political power of the South in Congress during Reconstruction and after. This meant that the expanded black vote became necessary to the North as a loyal, anti-white Democrat, pro-Republican counterforce on the Southern scene. To the New South, black enfranchisement was something to be curtailed, but the increased representation counted, just as it had under the three-fifths clause before the war. It took to the 1890s before that goal was fully accomplished, and the North gave up on trying to reconstruct the South, until 60 years into the 20th century.

Legislature. But the damage was done. In control of one house of Congress, the Republicans were on the march to a presidential electoral victory in 1860, with only 39% of the popular vote.[87]

No one was fooled by Lincoln's first inaugural speech. No interference with slavery in the states, indeed! The Democrats in the North accused the Republicans of trying to get around the constitutional guarantees on slavery by acting indirectly against the South by nibbling at the edges of the slave system, attacking the domestic and international slave trade, and refusing to enforce the fugitive laws.

Southern Secessionist Democrats said much the same, calling the Cordon of Freedom an "inflammatory circle of fire." The spearhead would be more domestic insurrections inspired by would-be John Browns. Southern cooperationists, those who opposed immediate secession, had no quarrel with the Democrats. But Southern cooperationists and Northern Democrats pointed out that, if the South were to leave the Union, it would lessen the Democrats' political power in Congress and negate Republicans' obligation to obey the Constitution or any laws protecting slavery. Secession would lead to direct invasion and the imposition of immediate Military Emancipation, the second part of the Republican policy against slavery. Indeed, Republicans might actually favor Southern secession through which to attack the slave institution at once. Even the slaves understood this—they hoped for secession and invasion to end their enslavement posthaste.

Until now, historians of all stripes ridiculed these stated policies as being in error. Historians have called the Northern Democrats demagogues, the Southern secessionists hysterical,

---

[87] William W. Freehling, *The Road to Disunion II: Secesionists Triumphant* (New York: Oxford University Press, 2007), 323. See also, in general, Brenda Weinapple, *Ecstatic Nation:Confidence, Crisis, and Compromise, 1848-1877* (New York: Harper, 2013).

and the slaves misguided. After all, Lincoln promised to protect slavery where it existed in the states in his inaugural address, didn't he? The Republicans and their President waited until 1863 to attack slavery, didn't they?

But what if the historians are wrong and the secessionists were correct? What if Lincoln and the Republicans intentionally refused to compromise the one issue that could have postponed the war; namely, the spread of slavery in the territories that Chief Justice Taney ruled as constitutional in the Dred Scott case? What if Lincoln and the Republicans decided to forget the Cordon of Freedom and proceed directly to Military Emancipation? What if Lincoln and the Republicans misjudged how long a Civil War might last and how fiercely the South would fight to maintain its social, cultural and economic institutions? What if the Republicans began to attack slavery even before Lincoln was inaugurated and, with the new President's connivance, never relented?[88]

The place to look for this plot to effect immediate Military Emancipation is not at the machinations leading up to the firing on Ft. Sumter as most historians do, but rather during the "Winter of Secession," prior to Lincoln's inauguration, in the U.S. Senate's Committee of Thirteen, designed to compromise the slavery issue once again, chaired by John J. Crittenden of Kentucky. Crittenden was a compromiser in the style of his mentor Henry Clay—who, oddly enough, was Lincoln's mentor, too.

But while Crittenden, like Clay, was a healer interested in mitigating the sectional controversy, Lincoln was more interested in Clay's economics, using the Federal government to promote industrialism and rid America of slavery. What Crit-

---

[88] Oakes, "Was the Civil War Actually about Slavery?" [3]. For a full discussion of Military Emancipation historically, see Oakes, *Scorpion's Sting*, 104-65.

tenden and his committee proposed was a modification of the Missouri Compromise—even though Justice Taney and the Supreme Court had ruled the original unconstitutional in Dred Scott. The new plan was to extend the 36-degree 30-foot line to the eastern border of the free state of California. Slavery was to be protected in the West in all territory possessed by the United States at that time and also "hereafter acquired" below the Missouri Compromise line

Crittenden thought that reasonable. But there was a quirk in the process—a critical procedural rule in the committee. The proposal would have to be endorsed by a majority of Democrats in the committee, and a majority of Republicans, too. Key Southerners on the committee thought Crittenden's plan acceptable. Conservative Democrat Jefferson Davis gave it his support. Robert A. Toombs, a red-hot secessionist, was against Crittenden's proposal, but he thought voters back home in Georgia would accept it. So he voted in favor with Davis. Other Democrats followed suit.

But the five Republicans on the committee would have none of this. Crittenden's plan would break the Cordon of Freedom around the South. Especially objectionable was the phrase, territory "hereafter acquired." This smacked of encouragement of Southern pseudo-military filibustering expeditions throughout the Caribbean to acquire more slave territory below the Missouri Compromise line. Led by William H. Seward, the Republicans on the Crittenden Committee voted *en masse* not to accept the Compromise. The secessionist fire-eaters in and out of Congress were more than happy with the result. They brooked no compromise, either.[89]

---

[89] How the slightly differing viewpoints merged is explained in Robert J. Cook, William L. Brney, and Elizabeth R. Varon, *Secession Winter: When the Union Fell Apart* (Baltimore: The Johns Hopkins University Press, 2013), 1-9, 86-90; Charles B. Dew, *Apostles of Disunion: Southern Secession Commissioners and the Causes of the Civil War* (Charlottesville: University

Nor did Abraham Lincoln. Actually, the key question is, "Why did Lincoln end up such a no-compromise hard-liner?" Lincoln historians say it was because he was adhering to the Republican Platform of 1860. Maybe.[90] But that is actually hindsight. What Lincoln's position really reveals is that he was probably more in league with the Radical Republicans that historian have been willing to admit until recently.

More importantly, other historians believe that Lincoln's no-compromise position demonstrated his ignorance of the South. Lincoln, like most Northerners, had heard all this secession braggadocio in 1798, 1832, 1850, and incessantly for the past few years. They all believed that it was nothing but drivel spouted by a few loudmouths soon to be put down by sensible Union men all over the South, as it had been in 1850.

The record indicates that by 1860, Lincoln was no longer a Border State Southerner, but had internalized the common Northern antislavery image of the South. It was a society of rudely domineering, rich planters, and cowering non-slaveholding yeoman farmers. The average Southerner, believed Lincoln, was like Lincoln himself, a conservative unionist with little attachment to slavery, whose family had fled the South of slavery when he was but a boy. This is what Lincoln and the Republicans saw, so the South had little to fear from their Cordon of Freedom or even Military Emancipation. Pro-slave secession would fold in a minute before the might of such Southern freeholders.[91]

Press of Virginia, 2001).

90 In another vein, economist Walter Williams exhorts us "to follow the money." He correctly asserts that before the Civil War, tariffs and excise taxes were 90% of Federal income. In 1859, for example, the Southern ports paid 75% of all such expenses. No responsible politician could let that much revenue go through allowing secession, regardless what the Constitution might say. See Williams, "Abe Lincoln's Hypocrasy," at www.wnd.com/ author/willians/2015/07.

91 William J. Cooper, "The Critical Signpost on the Journey toward Secession," *Journal of Southern History*, 77 (No. 1, February 2011), 16. The contrary view of Lincoln as perpetual and sympathetic Southerner, is in James G. Randall, *Lincoln and the South* (Baton Rouge:

If the Southern slaveholders could not understand this, well then, they could simply leave the Union, and accept invasion and eventual subjugation and seizure of their slave property. They would no longer have the protection they had once enjoyed from the Constitution, the rulings of the U.S. Supreme Court, or the laws of Congress, up to now made possible by an unjust Slave Power Conspiracy.[92]

So, the South took up Lincoln's suggestion in December 1860 and seven states seceded by February 1861. All Lincoln needed now was to conceal the real reason for an armed conflict by goading the South into firing the first shot and calling the nation together to avenge this insult to the American flag. It took place at Ft. Sumter, South Carolina. Three-quarters of a million dead Americans later (8 million in proportion to current population), including the Yankee president himself, Lincoln's suppositions proved completely wrong. The South had fought at last, slaveholders and freeholders united, with tremendous fury.[93]

But Lincoln got his Military Emancipation. It started just like he and his Republican Party pledged, immediately. On May 23, 1861, three slaves engaged in what black historians like to call an act of "self-emancipation" by rowing across Hampton Roads to Fortress Monroe, Virginia, held by Union forces. They asked for asylum. The commandant of the fort was General Benjamin F. Butler of Massachusetts, who declared the refugees to be "contraband of war," and refused to return them to their owner as the Fugitive Slave Act of 1850 demanded. By August 11, Congress had passed the First Confiscation Act, confirm-

---

Louisiana State University Press, 1946).

92 Oakes, "Was the Civil War Actually about Slavery?" [4].

93 See, James M. McPherson, "What Caused the Civil War?" *North & South*, 4 (November 2000), 12-22; Jeffrey R. Hummel, "Why Did Lincoln Choose War?" *ibid.*, 4 (September 2001), 38-44; Webb Garrison, *Lincoln's Little War* (Nashville: Rutledge Hill Press, 1997); Thomas J. DiLorenzo, *The Real Lincoln*, 89-125.

ing that slaves fleeing "disloyal" masters could be forfeit to the United States.

Soon after, General John C. Fremont, the Republican presidential candidate in 1856, freed the slaves of all disloyal persons in his command area, Missouri. General David Hunter followed soon after in Fremont's policy by putting it into effect in his command area along the occupied coast in South Carolina. Lincoln disallowed both proclamations, fearing their adverse affect in the loyal un-seceded Border States, but Congress passed a Second Confiscation Act in July 1862, which freed all slaves in Rebel areas of the South—if they could but get to Union lines.

Sometimes the Union lines came to the slaves. General Butler continued his emancipation in the newly captured city of New Orleans and parts of Southeastern Louisiana. Several of his subordinates raised black regiments, called "Corps d'Afrique" in Louisiana patois, made up of ex-slaves and freedmen, for the Union cause. But to put the freedom section of the Second Confiscation Act into effect, Congress had instructed the President to issue a proclamation saying so.[94]

Lincoln delayed his presidential order until the Yankees had won a battle at Antietam, Maryland, turning back a Confederate invasion of the North. Then he issued a preliminary Emancipation Proclamation to put the freedom sections into effect. The preliminary Emancipation Proclamation gave the Confederates 100 days to come back into the Union or else Lincoln would free all slaves in the Confederacy.

Hearing nothing from Southern government leaders, on January 1, 1863, the Northern President as promised issued the permanent Emancipation Proclamation, the Republican

---

94 *An Act to Suppress Insurrection, to Punish Treason and Rebellion, to Seize and Confiscate the Property of Rebels, and for Other Purposes (July 17, 1862)*, Public Acts of the 37th Cong., 2nd sess., ch. cxcv, sect. 5. See also, John Syrett, *The Civil War Confiscation Acts: Failing to Reconstruct the South* (New York: Fordam University press, 2005).

Congress' Military Emancipation writ large, freeing all slaves in the Confederacy (but not in the whole Union).

The four un-seceded border slave states still refused to go along with any form of emancipation. Finally, Lincoln and the Republicans got western Virginia in Wheeling to "secede" from disloyal Virginia at Richmond, with the approval of so-called loyal Virginia at Alexandria. At Congress' insistence, part of West Virginia's application for statehood included an emancipation provision for the new state. Republican electoral takeovers of Missouri and Maryland soon followed, with their own ensuing state-ordered, uncompensated emancipations.

But Kentucky and Delaware continued to refuse to free their slaves. Since all Military Emancipation was a wartime measure there was some doubt as to its enforcement after the war was ended. This meant that all of the congressional and presidential emancipations might be declared null and void. So in a bit of irony, President Andrew Johnson, having succeeded the martyred Lincoln, made readmission of the South into the Union conditional upon their acceptance of the proposed Thirteenth Amendment, much tougher than any Reconstruction program that Lincoln had introduced during the war.[95] This ended slavery as involuntary servitude, although Kentucky and Delaware refused to ratify the amendment until the twentieth century (in 1976 and 1901 respectively), but Charles Sumner's dream of Freedom National had become nation-wide at last on December 18, 1865.[96]

But while this accepted story of Lincoln's establishment of Freedom National seems valid, there is another theory of what was at stake here. It fits right in with "Miz Milly" Rutherford

---

95 Thomas, *The Reason Lincoln Had to Die*, 2.
96 Oakes, *Freedom National, passim*.

and John Wilkes Booth's assertion that Lincoln started the war on purpose.

In a review of Richard Brookhiser's new book, *Founder's Son: A Life of Abraham Lincoln*, noted Civil War scholar and current president of Harvard University, Drew Gilpin Faust takes the author to task, challenging the notion that Lincoln was backward looking to the Declaration of Independence, the Constitution of 1787, and the reestablishment of the old Union. She much prefers the idea of Garry Wills in his tome, *Lincoln at Gettysburg*, that the sixteenth president was futuristic and precedent-breaking, looking to "create a new nation," as he put it, "conceived in Liberty, and dedicated to the proposition that 'all men are created equal,'" which he called "a new birth of freedom."[97]

This "new nation" idea was presented even more forcefully as the thesis to Steve Berry's new novel, *The Lincoln Myth*.[98] A lawyer from Atlanta, Berry has traded the intricacies of jurisprudence to approach the constitution and law with a common touch and a fictional adventure story to titillate the palates of those less sophisticated than professional historians.

Unlike the 1781 Articles of Confederation, which were self-described as perpetual, Berry points out that the Constitution of 1787 and its amendments never said that the United States was established for perpetuity. Nowhere did the Constitution prohibit Secession or speak of perpetuity. Instead, it spoke of a "More Perfect Union." The States never lost the right to secede from the United States under the Constitution of 1787, says Berry, any more than Colonies lost it in seceding from Britain.

---

97 Richard Brookhiser, *Founder's Son: A Life of Abraham Lincoln* (New York: Basic Books, 2015); Drew Gilpin Faust, "O Captain!" *The New York Review of Books* (Sunday, February 8, 2015), 1, 19; Garry Wills, *Lincoln at Gettysburg: The Words that Remade America* (New York: Simon & Schuster, 1992); Basler (ed), *The Collected Works of Abraham Lincoln*, VII, 17-23, especially 23.

98 Steve Berry, *The Lincoln Myth* (New York: Ballentine Books, 2014), 131-35, 170-73, 301, 420, 484-87.

Indeed, New York, Virginia, and Rhode Island reserved the right of secession when they ratified the new Union under the Constitution of 1787. No one complained at the time about those reservations, Berry correctly asserts. Indeed, the South threatened secession in 1798, 1832, and 1850, before it did so in 1860. The North threatened to secede in 1814. Some abolitionists saw secession as a viable option, too.

When did the notion of a Perpetual Union begin? Berry maintains it happened when Lincoln announced it in his First Inaugural speech in 1861. The key is that Lincoln did not, as most historians say, preserve an indivisible Union. He fought to establish a Union that was to *become* perpetual. Nowhere in the Constitution of 1787 were the states prohibited from seceding. Indeed, they seceded from the Articles of Confederation to regain and maintain the right of secession. This was guaranteed in the Tenth Amendment, where it says that all powers not directly granted the Federal government were reserved to the individual States.

The States were important entities to the delegates of the Constitutional Convention. They were maybe even more important to their citizens (residents), Berry observed. That is the way Americans thought before the Civil War, much as Robert E. Lee held that he could not draw his sword against his native land, Virginia. It was not until 1861 that Lincoln changed that in his First Inaugural speech. To Lincoln, the States were never sovereign. He said that the Continental Congress created them, not the people. They were meaningless to him. He believed that, once made, any constitutional contract among the States was irrevocable.

Was Lincoln correct? Berry asked. Jefferson and Madison would have said "no." Lincoln had to choose. Save the United

States or let the individual States go free, as Buchanan and the Democrats wanted, according to the Constitution. The Southern States were already seceded. So Lincoln had to force them back into the Union, beginning a war that was disguised as a Southern Rebellion. [99]

John F. Kennedy once spoke of such the relationship between truth, myth, and history:[100]

> The greatest enemy of truth is often not the lie—deliberate, contrived and dishonest—but the myth—persistent, persuasive and unrealistic. Too often we hold fast to the clichés of our forebears. We subject all facts to a prefabricated set of interpretations. We enjoy the comfort of opinion without the discomfort of thought.

Our modern interpretations of Lincoln border more on a man of myth than fact. Alphonso Taft, U.S. secretary of war (1876), U.S. attorney general (1876-1877), and nineteenth century progenitor of the family that produced a slew of noted Ohio Republican politicians, understood what had to come. Taft wrote about the necessities of future history and the importance of myth in a letter to his home-state U.S. solon, Senator *pro tem* Benjamin Wade, on September 8, 1864:[101]

> "It is to be regretted that history should have to tell so many lies as it will tell, when it shall declare Lincoln's intrigues and foolishness models of integrity and wisdom, his weakened and wavering indecision and delay far-

---

99 Walter Williams, "The War of 1861: Brute Firce," www.wnd.com/2015/07/author/wiliams.
100 Kennedy's Yale Commencement Speech, June 11, 1962, quoted in Berry, *ibid.*, 470.
101 Alfonso Taft to Benjamin Wade, September 8, 1864, copy in David Rankin Barbee papers, Archives, Georgetown University, Box 3.

sighted statesmanship, and his blundering usurpation of legislative power Jacksonian courage and Roman patriotism, but one cannot help it. History goes with the powers that be."

The Perpetual Union Lincoln spoke of was something no one believed in 1861. States' rights ruled the heretofore. It is the Lincoln Myth. So, Berry's thesis in a nutshell is that Lincoln did not fight the Civil War to *preserve* the Union. He fought to *create* it, for the first time. In the words of Fawn Brodie, Lincoln and the Republicans "pushed vigorously toward the consolidation of the federal power, and helped transform what was a sprawling, invertebrate country into what a unified nation, responsive to strong central leadership."[102] And it was all quite intentional, as was the war that initiated this new Nation.

Berry's thesis that a perpetual union was the result of the Civil War is echoed in different words by constitutional scholar Akhil Reeed Amar in his recent book, *The Law of the Land*. Amar asserts that Lincoln through his wartime polices so changed the Union, that we now live not in the country created by the Founding Fathers, but one better characterized by the slogan on the vehicle license plates of the State of Illinois: "The Land of Lincoln."[103]

It only remained for the U.S Supreme Court to declare the new Land of Lincoln legal and constitutional. This happened in 1869 in the case Texas v. White.[104] The Court ruled that secession was illegitimate and that all laws passed during the rebellion by any seceded State, which promoted the Confederacy, were illegal and unconstitutional *ab initio*, i.e., from their inception.

---

102 Fawn M. Brodie, *Thaddeus Stevens: Scourge of he South* (New York: Norton, 1966), 370.
103 Akhil Reed Amar, *The Law of the Land: A Grand Tour of Our Constitutional Republic* (New York: Basic Books, 2015)3-28, 307-12.
104 Texas v. White (April 12, 1869), 74 U.S. (7 Wall.) at 700.

What was the Supreme Court to do? Declare the whole Civil War unconstitutional?

Besides, to admit the veracity of secession would have made the War of the Rebellion exactly what the South called it—a War for Southern Independence or War of Northern Aggression. So Lincoln and the Republicans began the War of Northern Aggression, which they, the Supreme Court, and historians ever since have disguised as the War of Southern Rebellion, the official name of our Civil War. Lincoln and the Republicans "deliberately and personally conceived," a "new Nation" through an aggressive war of conquest and made it perpetual at last, forever. Oddly, it was a process that Lincoln had predicted would happen when he was an unknown attorney in his 1838 speech to the Young Men's Lyceum at Springfield, Illinois, "whether at the expense of emancipating slaves, or enslaving freemen."[105]

---

105 Basler (ed.), *The Collected Works of Abraham Lincoln*, I, 108-15. The significance of Abraham Lincoln's 1838 Speech before the Young Men's Lyceum is laid out in Edmund Wilson, *Patriotic Gore: Studies in the Literature of the American Civil War* (New York: Oxford University Press, 1962), 106-108. A more recent look ad the speech is Major L. Wilson, "Lincoln and Van Buren in the Steps of the Fathers: Another Look at the Lyceum Address," *Civil War History*, 29 (September 1983), 197-211. Also important are the materials in George B. Forgie, "Lincoln's Tyrants," in Boritt, Gabor S, and Norman O. Furness (eds.). *Historian's Lincoln: Pseudohistory, Psycohistory, and History* (Urbana: University of Illinois Press, 1988, 285-312. Forgie wonders whether Jefferson Davis and others of the same era saw a similar threat to American institutions as did Lincoln, and reacted just as dictatorially as he has been accused of doing.

III.

GEORGE N. SANDERS

A Professional Revolutionary for Manifest Destiny, an Independent Confederacy, and Worldwide Constitutional Government

Of all the known Confederate agents in Montreal, British Canada East, only one was easily recognizable as the famous, or infamous, as many on both sides of the Civil War tended to see him, George N. Sanders. Too lazy to shave and clean himself and an out-and-out blackguard went the cant. And he had one really big fault for a spy or quasi-secret agent—Sanders just could not keep his mouth shut, any time, anywhere.

He commonly wore a dark suit that was obviously soiled with light streaks of dust that emphasized its numerous wrinkles and was always in need of a good brushing. His white shirt had not seen an iron at all, and one shirttail was often outside his trousers, hanging from under his waistcoat, visible between the folds of his unbuttoned coat. His cravat hung carelessly and lopsidedly, but his long, shaggy, untrimmed black beard covered most of that. Sanders regularly crossed the great iron bridge at Niagara Falls in the disguise of being a Cornish miner. He really did not need much camouflage to achieve that role readily.

Whenever Sanders had eaten, remnants of each course stuck

to the hairs around his lips. Indeed, as his yellow, smoke-stained, food-filled teeth showed when he grinned, all Sanders needed to make his next meal was a good toothpick. But at least he was not a drunk, as his unkempt appearance suggested from a distance. Yet despite his unattractive social graces, one felt drawn to Sanders. His glass-blue eyes were almost beautiful. His voice and attitude were magical.[106]

Born at what became Lexington, Kentucky, on February 21, 1812, George Nicholas Sanders was descended from some important Virginia forbearers. These included Robert "King" Carter, one of the biggest slaveholders of the colonial era, and Lewis Sanders, an instigator with James Madison of the Kentucky Resolves that asserted a state's right to nullify any unwise federal law (in this case the Alien and Sedition Acts of 1798) they deemed unconstitutional, three years before John Marshal reserved that privilege for the U.S. Supreme Court alone in the famous case, Marbury *v.* Madison. Lewis Sanders also had supported Aaron Burr's attempts to separate the American West from the then dominant states of the Eastern seaboard.[107] Political radicalism ran deep in Sanders' blood.

Sanders grew up in a commercial family that moved into the Kentucky interior after the War of 1812 and became prominent in raising grain crops and livestock at the farm, "Grass Hills." As he matured, George became a noted livestock breeder and dominated local racetracks and cattle trading through his innate

---

[106] Short to moderate-sized sketches on George N. Sanders can be found on the web through any search engine. For a reliable, short, scholarly look at Sanders, see Merle E. Curti, "George Nicholas Sanders," in Dumas Malone (ed.), *Dictionary of American Biography* (New York: Charles Scribner's Sons, 1935), XIV, 334-35. A more recent look at Sanders is Higham, *Murdering Mr. Lincoln*, 21-50.

[107] The definitive work on Sanders is the sadly unpublished manuscript by Randall A. Haines, "The Notorious George N. Sanders: His Career and role in the Lincoln Assassination" (unpublished ms. in the James O. Hall Library, Surratt House Museum, 1994). For material in this and the succeeding paragraphs on Sanders' early life, courting his true love, and Democratic, expansion politics, see *ibid.*, 62-115, 131. Most other commentators give Sanders' birth date as February 22, but we chose to go with Haines, his Boswell

skill in both fields. His education was through private schools, and there is still some dispute as to whether he attended college. But regardless of a college education or not, he was an intellectual who read widely.

One of the many magazines he read was a New York publication, *Passion Flower*. Its editor was a young Anna J. Reid, with whom George engaged in a platonic letter-writing exchange that soon blossomed into a more intimate tête-a-tête. They swapped discreet articles of clothing (it was before photos were readily available)—his vest and her slipper. True love could not be denied. He was off to New York City with his father in tow, and three days after meeting Anna, they were married, a union that proved happy and produced three sons (Reid, Lewis, and George, Jr.) and one daughter (Virginia).

It seemed not to bother Anna one iota that George N. Sanders made a career out of supporting so-called radical ideas in the middle nineteenth century. He was one of the first to push for the securing of Texas during the 1844 presidential campaign. An original backer of James K. Polk, along with Democratic strategist, Robert Walker of Mississippi (via New York), Sanders developed the notion that Polk should campaign for the *re*-annexation of Texas, implying that the United States really should have had it from the old Adams-Onís Treaty with the Spanish back in 1819. He called for the *re*-annexation of Oregon, too, to keep the North happy. These territories were all part of the original Louisiana Purchase went the tale and America had been cheated out of them. After the Oregon Treaty with Great Britain gained the U.S. everything south of the forty-ninth parallel, Sanders personally worked with the English Hudson's Bay Company to settle their claims against America, for a price, but he saw little from it.[108]

---

108 The Hudson's Bay Claims are treated in John S. Galbraith, "George N. Sanders:

But there were adverse political repercussions emanating from Sanders' plan, too. When Polk compromised with Great Britain at the forty-ninth parallel, the Yankees accused him, as a Southerner, mind you, of going soft on *their* opportunities to expand to the west. Oregon was then comprised of what the English now call British Columbia, the U.S. Territory of Washington, and what would become the American state of Oregon in the late 1850s.

The North was especially angry when Polk favored the movement to annex *all* of Mexico in 1848. The Mexicans had lost the war, was Polk's reasoning, and it would make for prime slavery expansion. The northern Mexican states were full of mines (those at San Luis Potosí, had produced gold and silver since the days of the *conquistadores*) and cattle (eventually one-third or more of the cowboys in Texas were black or Hispanic), while those Mexican states just below Texas and along the Gulf coast would support the South's standard plantation system of growing staple crops for export. North American slavery had great potential in Mexico, if the native *encomienda* (traditional forced labor system) was any indication.

But a measure called the Wilmot Proviso killed all that, because it called for no slavery in any territory taken from Mexico, even before the war of conquest started. The proviso passed the House of Representatives, aided by the influx of Northeastern settlers into the Old Northwest, the states around the Great Lakes, Iowa and Minnesota, that had made them more like New England in flavor, and affected the anti-slavery vote. But it failed in the evenly divided Senate.[109]

'Influence' Man for the Hudson's Bay Company," *Oregon Historical Quarterly*, 53 (September 1952), 159-76. The politics of the 1844 presidential election, the annexation of Texas (Sanders' brother had been killed in the Texas Revolution of 1836), and events preceding and following it are in Haines, "The Notorious George N. Sanders," 106-11; John Siegenthaler, *James K. Polk* (New York: Henry Holt & Co., 2004), 70-131.

109 The Wilmot Proviso and outcome of the War with Mexico is discussed in Chaplain W.

The failure of the annexation of all of Mexico stymied one of Sanders' favorite schemes—Manifest Destiny. Sanders' friend, John L. O'Sullivan, first published that phrase in his sheet, *The United States Magazine and Democratic Review*. Then Sanders and O'Sullivan got a hold of the notion of "Young America" that came out of South Carolina from writer and political theorist Edwin de Leon. He believed that nations had a life, just like people. Some were young, others middle aged, and others old.

Sanders and O'Sullivan made it sound prettier. "Nations, like men, have their seasons of infancy, manly vigor, and decrepitude." The United States was full of "exulting manhood," and Europe was worn out. Americans were on the rise; Europeans were in decline.

But contrary to Sanders' assertion, lots of young men in Europe decried their nations' impotency too, ruled as they were by corrupt kings and ministers, often from other ethnic groups. In 1848, young men throughout Europe created such organizations as Young Germany, Young Ireland, Young Hungary, and Young Italy. All were designed to overthrow the hereditary tyrants that had ruled Europe and subverted their own nations, often since Roman times. The rebels wanted to institute governments of their own, based on that of the United States or that of the early French Revolutionary Period, which was eventually devoured by Napoleon Bonaparte.

Sanders was thrilled. He was a born American revolutionary in the mold of 1776—even the idea of *constitutional* monarchy was a stench in his nostrils! He hopped the first ship for the continent. The would-be American rabble-rouser got to Paris in June 1848, helped construct the street barricades, imported

---

Morrison, *Democratic Politics and Sectionalism: The Wilmot Proviso Controversy* (Chapel Hill: University of North Carolina Press, 1967; Robert W. Merry, *A Country of Vast Designs: James K. Polk, the Mexican War, and the Conquest of the American Continent* (New York: Simon & Schuster, 2011).

guns from Samuel Colt's factory (but failed to get congressional financing as he wanted), and shouldered a musket for the revolution. Unfortunately, the insurrectionists could not beat the French regular army. Now upon the scene entered Napoleon's nephew, Louis, who proceeded to betray the whole revolution, compromising government by the people for his own corrupt ministers and his own absolute rule. To the dismay of Sanders and the rebels, Louis forsook democracy and constitution and quickly installed himself as the new Emperor of France as Napoleon III. Sanders' literary, drinking pal, Victor Hugo, called the new Emperor "Napoleon the Little," to distinguish him from his more famous uncle, "Napoleon the Great." Sanders preferred "Napoleon the Last," just to scare his fussy, effete majesty, the target of several attempted assassinations.

Sanders was among those who urged that the United States aid the new Republics in Europe, especially after the Russians crushed the Hungarians on behalf of the Austrians. That was when Louis Kossuth came to America for help. His appearance swept the popular imagination of United States citizens. Everyone was talking about him, and not just about his politics, but his sartorial splendor, and most particularly, his choice of headwear, the so-called "Kossuth" hat, which became popularly known and worn, as the "slouch" hat in America. But few Americans actually did anything. Not so George Sanders. He worked out a gun-running scheme for the Hungarians, just like he had for the French in 1848, but none of this came to fruition. Because of the blockades he couldn't get the guns to the Hungarians and too many American politicians said such action would violate the Monroe Doctrine, wherein Europe stays out of all of the Americas and the United States stays out of Europe's affairs.[110]

---
110   Haines, "The Notorious George N. Sanders," 123-31.

Sanders' disgust knew no bounds. With the assistance of newly-elected Illinois Senator Stephen A. Douglas, Sanders took over the old O'Sullivan newspaper. In exchange, he backed Douglas for president in 1852, and condemned the Democratic establishment as the "Old Fogies." These foot-draggers included old-time Jacksonian Democrats like Lewis Cass, William L. Marcy, John C. Breckinridge, James Buchanan, and even opposition party Whigs such as Henry Clay and Daniel Webster. The death of the last two after the Compromise of 1850 greatly helped Young America. With men like James Seddon, R. M. T. Hunter, Pierre Soulé, Robert Walker, James Shields, Daniel Sickles, and Douglas, Young America called for expansion and American democracy, expansion and progress, and hoped that the interest abroad would deaden the slavery controversy. But it only intensified the issue.

Unfortunately for the young iconoclasts, the Old Fogies managed to block Douglas' nomination in 1852, but the reformers slipped in Franklin Pierce, a quieter, more discreet representative of Young America, to be their candidate. He won the election and sent Sanders as consul and James Buchanan as minister to London, and Pierre Soulé as minister to Paris. Daniel Sickles was legation secretary to Buchanan, and he allowed Sanders to misuse the sanctity of the diplomatic pouch to communicate with fellow revolutionaries all over Europe. The Young Americans dressed in simple black to contrast themselves from the flashy European representatives, all of whom were dukes, earls, counts and lesser nobility. The Europeans laughed at the Americans and called them morticians. "We have come to bury monarchy," was the Americans haughty reply.

In those days, all of the exiled leaders of the Young you-name-it movements lived in London. Sanders issued invitations to all those who would come to assemble at his London home. And come they did. Louis Kossuth, Alexandre Ledru-Rollin, Arnold Ruge, Alexsander Herzen, Giuseppi Garibaldi, Giuseppi Mazzini, and Felice Orsini. Old Buchanan was so scared he asked Mrs. Sanders if she was not afraid that all the combustible materials about her would not blow up! But Old Buck came around to those "who had suffered in the cause of liberty," as he put it, and allowed one of the exiles, Victor Frondé (who wanted to kill Napoleon III) to be their official courier under a U.S. passport. When caught, Buchanan blamed it all on Sanders operating unsupervised behind his back.

Sanders did not care. He had published letters in the London press calling for Napoleon III's assassination, by any means, by any way. Everyone knew where he stood. But that and the failure in the U.S. Congress of the Ostend Manifesto, calling for the annexation of Cuba from Spain by hook or by crook, pretty well cooked his goose as consul, and that of his ally Soulé as Minister to France. Soulé resigned and the U.S. Senate never confirmed Sanders as consul. It was a recess appointment anyway, or *ad interim*, as the diplomats liked to say. The Old Fogies and the Republicans got Sanders, with some behind-the-scenes backstabbing by his one-time supporter, the erstwhile Senator Stephen A. Douglas. When angry, Sanders would refer to him as the "Young Giant," but came to see "Little Giant" as a much better title. More like "Napoleon the Little," thought Sanders.[111]

Things worsened, from Sanders' point of view, in the 1850s. With the admission of California as a Free State under the Compromise of 1850, there was no more slave territory within the United States in which the South could expand her institutions except the agriculturally unproductive desert Southwest between Texas and California. As the Wilmot Proviso demonstrated, the

---
111   *Ibid.*, 140-210.

North would block every move into Mexico or the Caribbean in the House of Representatives. As a result, Sanders' crony, Senator Stephen A. Douglas of Illinois, worked out a deal with Senator David Rice Atchison of Missouri and other Deep South Senators to open up Kansas and Nebraska in 1854 by repealing the Missouri Compromise restricting slavery to the territories south of 36°30' (the southern boundary of Missouri). The idea was that the South would get Kansas and the Yankees would take Nebraska. The people in the territories would decide the slavery question, and Douglas would become President. But the rapid influx of anti-slavery settlers from the North into Kansas, armed with breech-loading guns, which had been shipped in boxes marked 'Bibles,' stopped that.[112]

Sanders knew that it was important for the slave states to be able to exploit the West. If they could not send blacks into the West, the slave population threatened to overwhelm the whites in the South in a few decades. Already they outnumbered whites in South Carolina and Mississippi. Louisiana was not far behind. The Negroes birth rate was higher than whites living in the South. If the Republicans of the North set them free and made them citizens and voters the whole game was over. They would naturally vote Republican and eventually dominate every Southern state election in the future. The whites would have to leave their homes, or submit to black rule; leaving the homes their ancestors had established through blood and sweat where generations of their children had been born and raised.

Sanders, like many Southerners, turned his gaze from the

---

[112] The Compromise of 1850; the Kansas-Nebraska Act; and the Kansas-Missouri Border wars, and the eventual Kansas peace settlement are discussed in William L. Richter, *Historical Dictionary of the Old South* (Lanham, Md.: Scarecrow Press, 2006), 77-79, 200-207, respectively. For more detailed treatment, see also, Holman Hamilton, *Prologue to Conflict: The Crisis and Compromise of 1850* (New York: Norton, 1964) and James A. Rawley, *Race and Politics: "Bleeding Kansas and the Coming of the Civil War* (Philadelphia: Lippincott, 1969). The dry Southwest would not become agriculturally productive until the late 19th and 20th centuries, when the Native American's irrigation systems were modernized by Mormon settlers.

American West to the Islands of the Caribbean and the mainland of Central America. They sponsored extra-legal, military expeditions to conquer the Caribbean called "Filibusters" (a Spanish corruption of the Dutch word *frijbuter* or freebooter in English). William Walker was the moving force in this (the Gray-Eyed Man of Destiny, some called him), until he got himself executed down in Nicaragua. But others did the same in Baja California, Sonora, Chihuahua, the Yucatan, and Cuba, the last of the great sugar islands of the Antilles and a favorite target of the Filibusters especially after the Ostend Manifesto, as had the Wilmot Proviso before it, failed in Congress.

Sanders and other Southern expansionists were aghast at their failure and the lack of Northern support for Manifest Destiny. What an opportunity for a little *real* civilization at the point of a gun! A veritable Anglo-Saxon empire! Democratic Presidents like Polk, Franklin Pierce, and James Buchanan were with the South in spirit, but the anti-slavery Yankees blocked everything in the Congress.

The victorious North would change its mind in 1898 as the reunited nation went to war with Spain, and take possession of the Caribbean islands that would supply an expanding, jingoistic empire with a coaling station for its trading ships and the Navy that would protect them. But before the American Civil War, all Sanders and men like him had for public support was an 1841 novel by William Carruthers called *The Knights of the Golden Horseshoe*. It was about a passel of men, expansion-minded Southerners, who were devoted to expansion into the West and South in the Americas. Their emblem was a golden horseshoe.

In 1851, a magazine editor from Virginia named George W. L. Bickley, of whom Sanders was aware, created a real life organization modeled on the Golden Horseshoe which he called the Knights of the Golden Circle. His idea was to create a massive slave empire, centered on Cuba, and stretching from the American South through Mexico and Central America, over to Colombia and Venezuela into all of the Caribbean isles. The Knights soon had local chapters called "castles" all over the Northwest in areas below the old National Road (present-day U.S. Interstate Highway 70) and in the slave South.

But Sanders also knew that Bickley was a mere publicist. The real work was done by others, like Elkanah Greer, G. W. Chilton, Ben McCulloch, down in Texas, and Virginus Groener in Norfolk, Virginia. It might be said that the Golden Circle organized much of Texas secession, and helped mightily in Virginia, too.[113]

After secession, Sanders and Southern secessionists turned the castles in the Old Northwest into Copperhead outfits called the Order of American Knights. They had a newspaper published before the war in Maryland called "*The American Cavalier*. It promoted the Golden Circle politically, economically and culturally—an extension of the best part of America. The Knights would have brought the North in too, but the anti-slavery

---

113 On the Knights of the Golden Circle and Southern filibustering expeditions, consult Robert E. May, *The Southern Dream of a Caribbean Empire, 1854-61* (Baton Rouge: Louisiana State University Press, 1973), 3, 20, 49, 91-94, 148-55; Olliger Crenshaw, "The Knights of the Golden Circle," *American Historical Review*, 47 (1941), 23-50; C. A. Bridges, "The Knights of the Golden Circle: A Filibustering Fantasy," *Southwestern Historical Quarterly*, 287-302; and Joe A. Stout, Jr., *The Liberators: Filibustering Expeditions into Mexico, 1848-1862, and the Last Gasp of Manifest Destiny* (Los Angeles: Westernlore Press, 1973). Both John Wilkes Booth and neighbor T. William "O'Laughlen (if not his brother Mike, too, later a co-conspirator against Lincoln) were rumored to be members of the Golden Circle.

On Bickley, see James O. Hall, "A Magnificent Charlatan: George Washington Lafayette Bickley Made a Career of Deceit," *Civil War Times Illustrated.*, 18 (February 1980), 40-42; Edward Steers, Jr., "Who's Buried in Grant's Tomb?" *Surratt Courier*, 26 (April 2001), 5-7.

The Golden Circle's importance for secession and the Civil War is set out in an excellent article by Surratt Society member David Keehn, "Strong Arm of Secession: The Knights of the Golden Circle in the Secession Crisis of 1861," *North & South*, 10 (June 2005), 42-57. Keehn discounts the influence of the flamboyant Bickley in favor of others like Elkanah Greer, G. W. Chilton, Ben McCulloch, and Virginus Groener, generally ignored by modern historians. See also, Roy S. Dunn, "The KGC in Texas, 1860-1861," *Southwestern Historical Quarterly*, 70 (April 1967), 543-573, and Higham, *Murdering Mr. Lincoln*, 23, 28, 40, 47, 55-56, 65. 107, 113.

Yankees decried the Knights as part of what they saw as the Slave Power Conspiracy.

They called the U.S. Constitution that same thing—a Slave Power Conspiracy, guaranteed by the 1857 Dred Scott decision in the U.S. Supreme Court. Sanders and his allies were miffed. The North had squandered the opportunity of the century, he maintained, maybe even of the millennium!

The Golden Circle was typically American, Sanders believed. It advocated the expansion of the nation to encompass the whole North American continent and bring to it the blessings of American liberty and democracy through republican government under the Constitution as the Founders wrote it. This was the genesis of Sanders' New Mississippi Movement of 1857. It was designed to show the common interests of all those who lived in the Mississippi Valley or used the river system, regardless of their feelings toward slavery.[114]

This feeling was typified in the Louisiana secession movement when its convention passed a special proviso in its secession ordinance pledging to keep the Mississippi River open for Old Northwest commerce, but the state of Mississippi closed the river at Vicksburg, over its neighbor's protests. Sanders had hoped to get the secession of the Northwest or its adherence to the South in a trade alliance.[115]

In 1862, in conjunction with the preliminary Emancipation Proclamation, Sanders wrote a widely published article designed to appeal to the "Democratic Masses of the Mississippi Valley North." He used the ideas of a refugee named Karl Marx, whom

---

114 A really good summary of the Knights in the Old Northwest during the Civil War is in Bruce Catton, *Army of the Potomac: Glory Road* (New York: Doubleday, 1952), 111-24, *passim*. The Slave Power Conspiracy is discussed in Richter, *Historical Dictionary of the Old South*, 11-15, 299-302. See also, Merle E. Curti, "Young America,'" *American Historical Review*, 32 (October 1926), 34-55; Merle E. Curtis [sic], "George Sanders—American Patriot of the Fifties," *South Atlantic Quarterly*, 27 (January 1928), 79-87.

115 Richter, *Historical Dictionary of the Old South*, 293.

he had met in London. Sanders called on the Mississippi and Ohio Valleys to revolt from what he called the controlling capitalists of the Eastern states, who had elected Lincoln. He said correctly that Lincoln had forsaken his old home of Illinois for the New Birth of Freedom, a new Union of concentrated Federal power where, in the words of Lincoln's critics of his 1839 Speech to the Springfield Lyceum, the slaves would be freed and the free enslaved. "Organize! Organize for revolution!" Sanders said. "The independence of the State is the only safeguard against the centralizing and despotic instincts of the general government."[116]

Meanwhile, Sanders experienced the most crushing blow he had ever suffered when his son, Reid, a major in the Confederate army, was turned over to the Yankees by a so-called friend, who was in actuality a Federal agent. While attempting to run the blockade, Reid's ship was captured by a Federal gunboat, which was waiting for them in the fog. Imprisoned as a spy rather than a prisoner of war he withered away and died in Fort Warren a year later.[117]

In 1863, a vengeful Sanders was in Richmond negotiating with Confederate Secretary of State Judah P. Benjamin for a new courier system between the Confederacy and its representatives and agents in Canada employing blockade runners. He also spoke to President Davis about establishing an operation in Canada to work with the Yankee Peace Movement, the same program that took over the Democratic Party's presidential convention and became its platform in the election of 1864. Davis turned him down. Sanders left for Europe to help negotiate for Confederate ironclads to be built in England while his uncle by marriage, Richard Hawes, Jr., would-be Confederate governor

---

116 Haines, "The Notorious George N. Sanders," 354-56.
117 On Reid Sanders, see Meriwether Stuart, "Operation Sanders: Wherein Old Friends and Ardent Pro-Southerners Prove to be Union Secret Agents," *Virginia Magazine of History and Biography*, 81 (April 1973), 157-99.

of Kentucky, lobbied for the peace movement from Canadian bases until its adoption, in the aftermath of the Kilpatrick-Dahlgren Raid.[118]

Sanders knew that Davis was very cautious about interfering with Northern politics during the Civil War. But he was not totally oblivious to its potential. His first attempt to get in touch with these anti-Lincoln Yankees was when Davis sent Captain Emile Longuemare into the Old Northwest as early as 1862 to contact Democratic politicians and the old pre-war Knights of the Golden Circle. Like Longuemere, who was from Missouri, many of those involved in the Canadian Project were natives of the Border States; Kentuckians like Sanders and his in-law Richard Hawes, Jr., and Captain Thomas H. Hines and William Walter Cleary; and Marylanders, such as George P. Kane, and Patrick Charles Martin.

The idea was that border-staters "knew" Yankees better, especially Kentuckians like Sanders, who were the forebears of those who settled southern Ohio, Indiana, and Illinois, the centers of the opposition against Lincoln's war and domestic policies. And none was more important than Jefferson Davis, born in Kentucky, and although he grew up in Mississippi, he was educated in Kentucky at Transylvania College before he went to the Military Academy. Davis knew many of these men and their families, personally, and could recommend them all. These "Southern Yankees" had been friendly to Southern institutions and American expansion into Mexico and the Caribbean and Davis' agents were to assist in reorganizing them into the new Order of American Knights. Each group's inner circle (the men who could be counted on for armed and materiel support) was to be organized separately as the paramilitary Sons of Liberty.

As Sanders found out very quickly, these organizations were

---
118 Haines, "The Notorious George N. Sanders," 376-78, 400-403.

constantly exaggerating their power. The Republicans wanted to see them as strong to use them to discredit and arrest those Democrats who were against the war. The South wanted them to be strong to encourage others to join and to undertake armed offensive action. The Copperheads, or the Order of American Knights, wanted to be seen as strong to gain respect and power which they really did not have from Republicans and the Confederacy, and to impress possible future members.

While Sanders saw the contradictions between their outward and inner stances he knew they were not impotent. The Order implemented anti-draft riots, shootings of enrolling officers, encouragements of draft dodging; all undermining the Union war effort, from 1863 onward to the end of the war. The Confederates and their Copperhead allies put forth appropriate journalistic exaggerations of Union defeats on the battlefields with select editors and reporters, many of them members of the Order.[119]

By now, Sanders had had enough of what he saw as the half-way, milk-water sentiment of Jeff Davis and his government of Old Fogies. And so too, had Davis. With the Union Kilpatrick-Dahlgren cavalry raid on Richmond in early 1864, the Davis government decided to strike back at the North from behind their lines. The base of Confederate operations would be in British Canada, off limits to Union pursuit. These operations included forcibly freeing Confederate soldiers held in Northern prison camps, sabotage, assaults on Union territory from the

---

[119] In general, on Confederate agents and activities in Canada, see Haines, "The Notorious George N. Sanders," 424-538, and the very interesting separate article by Randall A. Haines, "Evidence of a Canadian Connection with Confederate Agents in the Lincoln Assassination." *Surratt Courier*, 29 (July 2004), 3-7. For more, see Tidwell, Hall, and Gaddy, *Come Retribution*, 20, 21, 328-34; "Booth in Canada," box 4, folder 221, DRB papers, GU. On Confederate Activities emanating out of the Canadian operation, see Jim Kushlan (ed.), "Rebel Secret Agents and Saboteurs in Canada," *Civil War Times Illustrated*, 40 (June 2001), [Special Issue]; Klement, *Dark Lanterns: Secret Political Societies, Conspiracies and Treason trials in the Civil War*, Higham, *Murdering Mr. Lincoln*, 116, 161-62; and James D. Horan, *Confederate Agent [Capt. Thomas H. Hines]: A Discovery in History* (New York: Crown Publishers, 1954).

relatively safe haven of British Canada, the instigation of disturbances against the Northern military draft, the introduction of infectious diseases into selected Union cities, the destruction of New York City by arson, and the blowing up of a portion of the White House during a cabinet meeting. All of these plots failed to achieve their goals, which pleased Sanders because he had opposed them from the beginning.[120]

More to Sanders' liking, the Confederates were to attempt a negotiated peace with the North on the basis of permanent separation of the old prewar Union. If this peace plan should fail, the Rebels were willing to look into the abduction of Lincoln (suggested by planter from Southern Maryland years earlier) or, failing at that, copy the Kilpatrick-Dahlgren plot (whose object had been to execute senior members of the Confederate government including Jefferson Davis) and thereby eliminate Lincoln and members of his cabinet. This assassination of Lincoln, "the theory of the dagger," as Giuseppe Mazzini called it in the Europe of the 1850s, was right down Sanders' alley. Indeed, if Sanders had his way, he would work the guillotine by steam, he said, and get all of the opponents of constitutional government, be they grasping monarchs or emperors, ineffective Old Fogies, or power-grabbing Republicans and their supporters, world-wide, in an assembly-line of destruction. [121]

As Sanders suspected all along, halfway measures did not work. The Niagara Falls Peace Conference fell apart as its sponsor,

---

120 The most authoritative source on Rebel behind-the-lines activities is Jane Singer, *The Confederate Dirty War: Arson, Bombings, Assassination and Plots for Chemical and Germ Attacks on the Union* (Jefferson, N.C.: McFarland & Co., 2005).

121 Haines, "The Notorious George N. Sanders," 255 (steam guillotine), 531 (failure of methods less than assassination). See also, Tidwell, Hall, and Gaddy, *Come Retribution*, 21-22, 24-25. David Rankin Barbee, "Lincoln and Booth" (unpublished manuscript, David Rankin Barbee papers, Archives, Georgetown University), 513-550, sees the Maryland connection as crucial. Maryland planters conceived the scheme to kidnap Lincoln as a solution to their own problems with Lincoln's policy (actually Congress' through the Confiscation Acts) of permitting their runaway slaves to be held without compensation as seized contraband of war, which the planters saw correctly as the beginnings of emancipation.

the easily manipulated reformer and do-gooder, Horace Greeley of the New York Tribune was replaced by the staunch Lincoln supporter, his private secretary John Hay. Captain Hay presented Sanders and the Confederates with a letter addressed cleverly "To Whom It May Concern." This refusal to credit Sanders and his cronies with any diplomatic status was accompanied with Lincoln's unwillingness to consider anything but a reunified United States as grounds for further discussion.

This was followed by a series of Rebel defeats on the battlefield from Atlanta to the Shenandoah Valley that ensured Lincoln's reelection in the North with Union soldiers leading the way as they voted from the front lines. Sanders managed to salvage some little success by getting the Canadian authorities to recognize the St. Albans, Vermont bank raiders not as common thieves, but as legitimate Confederate soldiers. Sanders' victory was made possible with documents brought all the way from Richmond by Sarah Slater, escorted partway by John Wilkes Booth's Maryland based co-conspirator, John Surratt. [122]

The way was now open for the 1848 European Revolutionaries' solution, the one favored by Sanders from the start—the assassination of, as the Confederate hard-liners saw it, the constitution-betraying dictator of the North, Lincoln himself. All Sanders needed now was a man to wield the dagger. Enter John Wilkes Booth. No one truly knows what went on between George N. Sanders and John Wilkes Booth in Montreal in October 1864. But Booth departed with an account in a Canadian bank frequented by Southern spies, letters of introduction to men like Dr. William Queen and possibly others,

---

122   Haines, "The Notorious George N. Sanders," 445-57, 458, 476, 489-516, 545, 548-49. For Surratt, see William L. Richter, *Confederate Freedom Fighter: The Story of John H. Surratt and the Plots against Lincoln* (Laurel, Md.: Burgundy, 2007).

and an introduction to Capt. Patrick Charles Martin, an expert blockade runner, who agreed to ship Booth's personal belongings and theatrical costumes to Richmond (they never arrived as the ship sank costing Booth his possessions and Martin his life).[123]

There remained but one other service for Sanders to perform for the Confederacy. He had to safeguard Confederate authorities from prosecution in Lincoln's death. Sanders saw one man as ideal for the job. As Sanders was well aware, Charles A. Dunham was a noted con-man. For men like Sanders and Dunham, the American Civil war was a windfall—politically and ideologically for Sanders, less nobly and more monetarily for Dunham. Both men operated on either side of the lines as occasion demanded. Dunham had used his time in Richmond, in prison or out, to learn much about the Confederacy. More important, he hung around various departments, purloining official copies of letterhead stationary. It was said that he could make it appear as if the Confederate government was operating out of any desk on the North American continent.

Sanders first saw Dunham loitering around the Niagara Peace Conference in 1864. He was supposedly a news reporter, using his expert knowledge to write articles on Confederate operations out of Canada. Like all reporters of the time, that which he could not divine, he simply made up out of whole cloth. Later, police picked him up while he was snooping around the U. S-Canadian border in the vicinity of St. Albans, Vermont, just after its banks had been liberated of their money by a group of Confederate raiders. He was arrested, but, encouraged by an informer, Canadian authorities soon found that he was harmless and turned him loose. His savior was none other than George N. Sanders.

---

123 Haines, "The Notorious George N. Sanders," 539-92, *passim*.

Sanders began to see great potential in Dunham, who was at the time writing articles for the *New York Tribune,* under the by-line of Sanford Conover. As usual, that which Dunham did not know, he fabricated. He also testified as an expert in the Canadian trial of the St. Albans raiders, authenticating the signatures of Confederate high officials, in this case, Secretary of War James A. Seddon. His testimony helped get the prisoners released, claiming that Confederate documents introduced to show them to be military men, and not mere robbers, were legitimate. This time, he used the name James Watson Wallace. By now, Sanders, who testified at the trial the same day as Dunham-Conover-Wallace, recognized that Dunham's incomparable talents, the big lie, forgery, aliases, false claims, and thievery, could be utilized on the behalf of the Confederate cause.

Essentially, what Sanders hired Dunham to do was to relate how the Confederates in Canada and Richmond planned and carried out the Lincoln assassination. It mattered not what he said or avowed as the truth. The legitimate Confederate agents denied everything and by the time the testimony was given at the trial of the co-conspirators, all of them Booth's friends and companions; no one really knew who was telling the truth and the whole matter became an improvable farce, as Sanders had wanted all along. Booth was dead; four of his closest allies went to the gallows, and three to Ft. Jefferson military prison in the Dry Tortugas off the coast of southern Florida. But Robert E. Lee, Judah P. Benjamin, John Surratt, John S. Mosby, George Sanders and others all cheated the hangman. [124]

---

124 On Sanders and the cover-up of Confederate participation in Lincoln's demise, see William A. Tidwell, *April '65: Confederate Covert Action in the Civil War* (Kent, Ohio: Kent State University Press, 1995), 148-54. For a contrary view of the Dunham story and his relation with Sanders, see Carman Cumming, *Devil's Game: The Civil War Intrigues of Charles A. Dunham* (Urbana: University of Illinois Press, 2008), 155-57. Yet for a history of how effective the cover-up was and how Sanders' scheme became the standard view of the assassination see, William Hanchett, "Lincoln's Murder: The Simple Conspiracy Theory," *Civil War Times Illustrated,* 30 (November/December 1991), 28-35, 70.

Sanders did not wait around to admire the success of his scheme. He soon returned to Europe after the war. Like John Surratt, he had a $25,000 price tag on his head, courtesy of President Andrew Johnson, and a group of Yankees had tried unsuccessfully to abduct him in Montreal that summer of 1865. He was involved in the revolt of the Paris Commune in 1872, supporting the communists under the red flag. He was on the losing side in that rebellion, too. Shortly afterward, he returned to the United States and lived out his life in obscurity. He died in New York and was buried in an unmarked grave in Greenwood Cemetery in Brooklyn [125]

Contrary to simplistic explanations as to the cause of the American Civil War (The War of The Rebellion as the North officially named it, The War For Southern Independence, as the South saw it), slavery had little to do with it. Sanders owned no slaves; he backed slavery not as a labor system but as a social system for division of the races. Sanders was instead a radical ideologue abroad and a conservative perfectionist at home, both with the same result in mind. He was a revolutionary for Manifest Destiny (forty years ahead of his time in the drive for American world empire, which occurred in 1898), an independent Confederacy (losing to superior force and Lincoln's destruction of the old Constitution of 1787 in his New Birth of Freedom),

---

The standard treatment of the charges against the Confederacy as perjured or the machinations of the evil mind of Union Secretary of War Edwin McM. Stanton are in David Miller Dewitt, *Assassination of Abraham Lincoln, passim*; Thomas R. Turner, *Beware the People Weeping*, 125-37, and Seymour J. Frank, "The Conspiracy to Implicate the Confederate Leaders in Lincoln's Assassination," *Mississippi Valley Historical Review*, 40 (Mar. 1954), 629-56.

For the testimony of Richard Montgomery, Sanford Conover (Dunham), and Dr. James B. Merritt, see Pitman (comp.), *The Assassination of President Lincoln and the Trial of the Conspirators*, 24-37. At least one trial commission officer believed the three told the truth, Harris, *Assassination of Lincoln*, 163-78, although W. W. Cleary, one of the Confederate mission in Canada denied it all for himself and the others, "The Attempt to Fasten the Assassination of President Lincoln on President Davis and Other Innocent Parties," *Southern Historical Society Papers*, 9 (July and Aug. 1881), 313-25.

125 Haines, "The Notorious George N. Sanders," 1-61.

and worldwide constitutional government (predating Woodrow Wilson's world vision at Versailles in 1919). George Sanders was *sui generis*—unique.[126]

---

126   Sanders' view was also why the common Confederate soldier fought for slavery, although a recent study suggests the Army of Northern Virginia had many more slaveholders among it enlisted ranks than supposed. See Kenneth M. Stampp, *The Peculiar Institution: Slavery in the Ante-Bellum South* (New York, Vintage Books, 1956), 32-33; Philip Katcher, *The Army of Robert E. Lee* (London, U.K.: Arms and Armour, 1994), 61-63; (Joseph T. Glatthaar, *General Lee's Army: From Victory to Collapse* (New York: Free Press, 2008), xiv. 19-20.

IV.

GUS HOWELL

Smarmy, Arrogant Blockade Runner and Murderer, or Effective-Behind-the-Lines Confederate Operative?

Ever since the 1988 publication of the landmark study of the Confederate Secret Service and its role in the Lincoln Assassination, *Come Retribution*,[127] the topic of Civil War spies and their contributions to the War effort has become a topic of increased interest among buffs and historians of the War for Southern Independence. Building upon pioneer works by such historians and popular writers historians such as James D. Horan, John Bakeless, Harnett T. Kane, Albert Castel, Merriwether Stuart, and John W. Headley,[128] more recent scholars including Alan Axelrod, E. C. Fishel, Jane Singer, Randall A. Haines, Edward Steers, Jr., Rick Stelnick, and Tidwell,[129] have probed the se-

---

[127] William A. Tidwell, James O. Hall, and David W. Gaddy, *Come Retribution: The Confederate Secret Service and the Assassination of Abraham Lincoln* (Jackson: University of Mississippi Press, 1988).

[128] James D. Horan, *Confederate Agent: A Discovery in History* (New York: Crown Publishers, 1954); John Bakeless, *Spies of the Confederacy* (Philadelphia: Lippincott, 1970); Harnett T. Kane, *Spies for the Blue and Gray* (Garden City, N. Y.: Hanover House, 1954); Albert Castel, "Samuel Ruth: Union Spy," *Civil War Times Illustrated*, 14 (February 1976), 36-45, and Meriwether Stuart, "Samuel Ruth and General R. R. Lee: Disloyalty and the Line of Supply to Fredericksburg," *Virginia Magazine of History and Biography*, 71 (January 1963), 35-109; Rick Stelnick, *Dixie Reckoning* (forthcoming); John W. Headley, *Confederate Operations in Canada and New York* (New York: Time-Life Books, 1984).

[129] Alan C. Axelrod, *War between the Spies: A History of Espionage during the Civil War* (New York: The Atlantic Monthly Press, 1992); Fishel, E. C., *The Secret War for The Union: The Untold Story of Military Intelligence in the Civil War* (Boston, Houghton Mifflin Co, 1996);

cretive, behind-the-lines activity of men and women on both sides—operatives Alan Pinkerton, Kate Warne, Walter W. Bowie, Rose Greenhow, Belle Boyd, John Yates Beall, Elizabeth Van Lew, Thomas W. Hines, Philip Henson, Sarah Slater, and George N. Sanders, to name but a few.

One of the hot-beds for spy activity was Southern Maryland, the area below of Washington, D.C., and Baltimore, stretching to the Potomac River. A center for wartime pro-Confederate sympathy, just how many Confederate agents existed in Maryland is hard to fathom, as recent scholarship by David W. Gaddy demonstrates.[130] But some Confederate operatives, while not invisible, usually went unnoticed by Yankee authorities as inconvenient gadflies, unless events demanded more attention. One such nuisance was Gus Howell.[131]

Born in Charles County at Bryantown in 1835, Howell was listed in the 1850 manuscript Federal census of Bryantown Election District as Gustavus, a farm laborer, aged fifteen years. Ten years later in the Manuscript census of 1860, he was again

---

Jane Singer, *The Confederate Dirty War: Arson, Bombings, Assassination and Plots for Chemical and Germ Attacks on the Union* (Jefferson, N.C.: McFarland & Company, 2005); Randall A. Haines, "The Notorious George N. Sanders: His Career and Role in the Lincoln Assassination" (Unpublished manuscript, in the James O. Hall Library, Surratt House Museum, Clinton, Md., hereinafter cited as JOH); Edward Steers, Jr., "Terrorism—1860's Style," *North & South*, 5 (May 2002): 14 ff; William A. Tidwell, *April '65: Confederate Covert Action in the American Civil War* (Kent, Ohio: Kent State University Press, 1995); James O. Hall, "Veiled Lady: The Saga of Sarah Slater," *North & South*, III (August 2000), 34-44.

130 See Gaddy's series of articles, "The Surratt Tavern—A Confederate 'Safe House'?" Kauffman (ed.), *In Pursuit of . . .* , 129-30; "Gray Cloak and Dagger," *Civil War Times Illustrated*, 14 (July 1975), 20-27; "William Norris and the Confederate Signal and Secret Service," *Maryland Historical Magazine*, 70 (Summer 1975), 167-88; and "John Williamson Palmer: Confederate Agent," *Maryland Historical Magazine*, 83 (Summer 1988), 98-110. Most illustrative as to how secret such activity could be is his "Confederate Spy Unmasked: An Afterward," *Manuscripts*, 30 (Spring 1978), 94. See also, Daniel L. Sutherland, "'Altamont' of the *Tribune*: John Williamson Palmer in the Civil War," *Maryland Historical Magazine*, 78 (Spring 1983), 54-66. For the familial ties of Howell and other Confederate agents in Maryland, see the excellent study by John Stewart, *Confederate Spies at Large: The Lives of Lincoln Conspirator Thomas Harbin and Charlie Russell* (Jefferson, N.C.: McFarland & Co., Inc., 2007), *passim*, especially 101-102.

131 Howell's habit of "flying under the radar" is evident in the standard, meager sketch of him in Edward Steers, *The Lincoln Assassination Encyclopedia* (New York: Perennial, 2010), 286-87.

listed, this time in Aquasco Election District Eight as twenty-four year-old Gustavus Howell, hotel keeper residing in Woodville, with a forty-five year old woman, Martha Curtis, presumably a slave, and her two children, both female ages eight and six, all black, listed as members of the household.[132]

Because of the Republican take-over of the U.S. House of Representatives in 1859 (made possible by the switch of Maryland representative Henry Winter Douglas from the Whig-American party to Republican party), and the election of Abraham Lincoln in 1860, the Lower South seceded in early 1861. The ensuing Republican majority in Senate of the United States, followed by the firing on Ft. Sumter and the secession of the Upper South, and Maryland's forceful retention in the Union after the Baltimore Pratt Street Riot, caused the pro-Southern Howell to cross the Potomac in June 1861 and joined a Confederate cavalry unit at Fredericksburg, Virginia, on the twenty-fifth of that month.

With Howell's enlistment in the Confederate army came a new issue—his name. All throughout the antebellum years, Howell seemed to be Gustavus Howell, or plain Gus. But his name as entered on his enlistment papers read: Augustus S. Howell. It was a low grade mystery that seemed of no account until he was compelled to testify at the military trial of the Lincoln assassination co-conspirators in 1865. But this mystery persisted during the war, too. When Mary Surratt introduced Howell to her nosy boarder, Louis Weichmann, she called him

---

132   The census leaves the question of miscegenation technically unanswered, but weighted in the negative, so far as census enumerator Thomas H. Harbin was concerned, or he would have listed the children as mulatto, the adopted convention in the South. See Federal Manuscript Census for 1850 (Maryland, Prince Georges County, Bryantown Election District, Federal Manuscript Census for 1860 (Maryland, Prince Georges County, Aquasco Election District #8), as excerpted by ancestry.com. Howell's Hotel is shown on the map of Woodville in Simon J. Martinet, *Martinet's Map of Prince Georges County, Maryland 1861* (Philadelphia: T. S. Wagner, 1861), 18. The picture of Howell's Hotel shown in his file in the William A. Tidwell papers, drawer 8, JOH, is incorrect—it actually portrays Harbin's Hotel in Piscataway.

"Mr. Spencer." Martha Murray, proprietress of the Herndon House, another Rebel boarding facility like Mary Surratt's in the District of Columbia, knew him as either Howell or Spencer, depending upon the occasion. The Confederate army knew him a Pvt. A. S. Howell. The Union knew him by various names and initials throughout the war.

During the Lincoln murder conspiracy trial, the Yankees wanted the absolute truth as regarded his name. Howell, to the astonishment of the judge advocate, said he really did not know! He admitted that he gave to the court the name A. S. Howell, "I believe." What did the Surratts call him? "My proper name, I suppose." What did A. S. stand for? "Augustus Howell." What was the S for? "Spencer." Was Spencer your name? "It is one of my many names," Howell retorted. "I was not particular in the name." Then he admitted his friends called him "Spencer," in the Southern manner of using middle names, rather than given ones. Well, the court wanted to know, what were you called in infancy, Augustus Spencer Howell? "I do not know," came the reply. Do you know your own name? "That is my name." Did you give that to the court? "I gave you the name of A. S. Howell," but Howell admitted he wrote it "short, A.S. Howell." Then he said he rarely used "Spencer." But he also used "Gustavus" occasionally. Finally the exasperated judge advocate asked what name he used to run the blockade. "Howell, generally" came the reply. Gus Howell definitely knew how to obfuscate the keenest Yankee lawyers with consummate skill.[133]

Waiting for horses and reinforcements that seemed never to come, A. S. Howell's company, led by Capt. R. Snowden Andrews, "seceded" from their parent unit and became the First Maryland Independent Battery of Artillery (CSA) or, as it was

---

133 Manuscript of the Testimony of Augustus S. Howell, 215-19, with Howell enclosures at ancestry.com

commonly known, the Baltimore Flying Artillery. There were four sections of two guns apiece (the unit had eight guns total, four Napoleon 12 pounders for close-in work and four 3 inch rifled guns for long-range fire) and Howell served in section two as a private, which meant he passed ammunition and helped load one of the Napoleons for firing.

The battery was stationed near Fredericksburg and helped the Confederates block free access up the Potomac until the Rebel army retreated to the Virginia Peninsula between the James and York rivers to defend Richmond, the new Confederate capital, from an invasion from Fortress Monroe by Maj. Gen. George B. McClellan's massive Army of the Potomac.

The First Maryland battery fought briefly with the Texas Brigade at Williamsburg and under Maj. Gen. James Longstreet at Seven Pines on the Nine Mile Road, where the battery was credited with displaying "extraordinary military tactics and heroism," a Civil War period euphemism for getting the living daylights knocked out of themselves by the enemy. These actions were the only battles in which Howell fought for Southern independence.[134]

As Howell and the Baltimore Flying Artillery joined Maj. Gen. A. P. Hill's "Light Division" on the front line as big gun support for the infantry in General Robert E. Lee's battles of the Seven Days, the Marylander became so sick from diarrhea that he was carried to the hospital on June 25, unable to move, much less fight. It was probably just as well. The Baltimore Flying Artillery was in the vanguard of the fighting and was shot to pieces, once again.

Meanwhile, Howell had physical problems of his own that would haunt him the rest of his life and lead to a premature death. On April 26, 1862 he was admitted to the Episcopal Hospital at

---
134 www.angelfire.com/md/freestaterebel/1stMD2.html.

Williamsburg with chronic diarrhea, a symptom of typhoid fever or "camp fever" as the Civil War surgeons described it. Typhoid fever was caused by salmonella typically spread by flies that flew from latrines to open food that was served to troops and for those who succumbed to it, resulted in the sufferer experiencing an especially putrid, green form of diarrhea called "pea soup" and dangerous dehydration. Since the Confederate army was retreating before McClellan's offensive thrust toward Richmond, Howell seems to have rejoined his battery for the delaying action fought at the city on May 5 and retreated to the battles around Richmond.

But in late June, just before Lee's offensive attack that marked the beginning of the Seven Days fighting, a battalion doctor sent Howell back to one of the military hospitals at Richmond. Here he received a diagnosis, in addition to the recurrent typhoid fever, of erysipelas, a serious bacterial skin infection, and phthisis, a fancy name for tuberculosis, known more commonly in the nineteenth century as consumption. Howell remained in the hospital until July 16, when he was discharged from the Confederate service because of "general disability." He received back pay of $129, less expenses.[135]

When Howell got back to Southern Maryland is not known, but he soon became involved in the popular pastime of funneling local Maryland recruits into the various companies, batteries, and regiments serving with Lee's Army of Northern Virginia. One of those engaged in the same activity about the same time was one George Malcolm Emack. Evidently Emack, a native

---

[135] Copies of Howell's medical and discharge papers are located in William A. Tidwell papers, drawer 8, JOH. The description of the diseases comes from Dr. Robert L. Smith, M.D., of Mills River, N.C. to Joseph E "Rick" Smith III, email sent July 24, 2011, in possession of the authors. For a period piece on the conditions facing Civil War soldiers like Howell, see Joseph K. Barnes and John Moore (comps.), *The Medical and Surgical History of the War of the Rebellion, 1861-1865* (3 pts., 6 vols., Washington: Government Printing Office, 1870-1888), especially Pt. 2, Vol.1 (*Medical History*, Diarrhea and Dysentery), Pt. 3, Vol. 1 (*Medical History*, Camp Fevers, etc.).

of Locust Grove in upper Prince Georges County, was picked up in lower Maryland by a roving patrol of Federal provost marshals (a common occurrence in that part of the state). While in the process of being escorted to the Old Capitol Prison in the District of Columbia, Howell was held for a short time at the T.B. Hotel, where he pulled out a concealed knife and stabbed one of his guards and broke free. The event was blamed on the man whose name Emack gave to his captors when arrested— his fellow recruiter and blockade-runner, Augustus Howell. It was an event which continuously erroneously to plague Howell's reputation to this present day.[136]

Howell's fortunes worsened on October 24, 1862, when Federal naval personnel of the U.S. schooner, *Matthew Vassar*, arrested him and five others while they crossed the Potomac. Howell was accused of "transporting rebels from Maryland to join the rebel Army" and as a result was lodged in the Old Capitol Prison. He was released on parole and rearrested on January 29, 1863, at Upper Marlboro for parole violation— essentially meaning he was doing more recruiting and blockade running. This time, in just a matter of weeks, Howell managed to get Col. Lafayette C. Baker, whose detectives had arrested him, to exchange him for a prisoner of equal value held by the Confederates.[137]

---

136 Emack's life story is revealed in the in Federal Manuscript Census for 1850 (Maryland, Prince Georges County, Bladensburg District), 1860 (Maryland, Prince Georges County, First [Beltsville] District), and 1880 (Kentucky, Woodford County, Versailles District), as excerpted by ancestry.com. A good biography of Emack, a much decorated officer in the First Maryland cavalry and a feared provost marshal at Castle Thunder Prison in Richmond, is at findagrave,com. Present-day correspondence and further information on Emack can be found at Lincoln-Assassination.com, Discussions, All Things Lincoln Assassination, topic: Augustus Howell and Emack.

137 James O. Hall, "The Saga of Sara Slater [orig., "Lady in the Veil," *Maryland Independent* (Waldorf), June 25, July 2, 1975]," in Michael W. Kauffman (ed.), *In Pursuit of* . . . (Clinton, Md: The Surratt Society, 1990), 69-88 at 78. See the letters from U.S. Provost Marshal, Seventh District of Maryland, Phelby Clark, January 24, 30, 1863, to Col. Lafayette C. Baker, concerning expenses needed to pay witnesses against Howell, drawer # 8, Tidwell papers, JOHRC.

After his prison stint, Howell went back to what he knew best, running the blockade. Evidently he collected drafts (checks) from Maryland soldiers who wanted them sent home to wives and families. For a fee, Howell crossed the Potomac and deposited the checks of the designated parties to their bank accounts. The Confederate government took special note of Howell's abilities as a trusted and effective blockade runner and assigned him to escort their premier female operative, Sarah Slater as she carried dispatches between Richmond and Montreal, the Confederacy's secret service headquarters in Canada.[138]

It was in this capacity that Howell is best known to modern Lincoln Assassination readers.[139] Escorting Slater, he traveled with her to New York City and returned to the Surratt townhouse in Washington, D.C., to await her return from Canada and a summons to meet her in downtown Manhattan. While awaiting Slater's summons, Howell stayed at Surratt's and, while there, met the ubiquitous, nosy busybody, and self-confessed Confederate sympathizer, Louis Weichmann. While Howell and Weichmann traded lies with each other, Howell taught him a simple box code cipher used by both sides to codify messages of lesser importance. Weichmann claimed that he used it to code and decode poems with a fellow clerk at the War Department's

---

138 See *ibid.*, 66-88, and Hall, "Veiled Lady: The Saga of Sarah Slater," 34-44; and Tonia Smith, "[Sara Slater]," (August 17, 1997), at users.nbn.net/tj1. The newest and most intriguing interpretation of Sarah Slater is John F. Stanton, "Some Thoughts on Sarah Slater," *Surratt Courier*, 32 (February 2007), 3-6. Stanton has at last located and clarified Slater's later life. See Lincoln-Assassination.com, Discussions, All Things Lincoln Assassination, topics: Slater/Surratt Relationship; the Lady in the Veil.

139 See, *e.g.*, Tidwell, Hall, and Gaddy, *Come Retribution*, 213, 415; Lloyd Lewis, *The Assassination of Lincoln: History and Myth* (Lincoln: University of Nebraska Press, 1994), 200; Charles Higham, *Murdering Mr. Lincoln: A New Detection of the 19th Century's Most Famous Crime* (Beverly Hills: New Millennium Press, 2004), 194, 200-201; Kauffman, *American Brutus*, 168, 192, 209; Kate Clifford Larson, *The Assassin's Accomplice: Mary Surratt and the Plot to Kill Abraham Lincoln* (New York: Basic Books, 2008), 56, 57, 58, 59, 72, 73, 126, 154, 212; William L. Richter, *The Last Confederate Heroes: The Final Struggle for Southern Independence & The Assassination of Abraham Lincoln* (2 vols., Laurel: Burgundy, 2008), I, 286-88, 341, 345-48; II, 10, 20, 37-38, 102-103, 235, 360, 365.

Office of Prisoner Exchange, where they were employed. Howell maintained that Weichmann used it to convey confidential messages concerning numbers and conditions of Confederate soldiers held in Northern prison camps.

In late March, Howell was at the Surratt Tavern a dozen miles below the District while waiting for Slater to return. The Confederates had been worried that Howell was being watched by Federal detectives and in danger of being arrested along with Slater. So in Howell's place, John H. Surratt, Jr., was sent to New York City to pick up and escort Slater to the tavern. Then Howell would take her the rest of the way to Richmond. To help Surratt identify her (she was exceedingly beautiful, and Surratt's heart throbbed with the very thought of being close to her as did most men's) she stood in front of A. T. Stewart's Department Store (one of the first and finest in the country and patronized by the likes of Mrs. Mary Todd Lincoln), carrying a horsehair switch which she held intertwined though alternate fingers.[140]

But when Surratt and Slater got to the tavern below Washington, his mother announced that Gus Howell had been arrested at the tavern on March 25, the evening before, and taken to the Old Capitol Prison once again. This circumstance forced Surratt to escort her all the way to Richmond, much to his prurient pleasure ("I have women on the brain," he confessed to livery stable owner Brooks Stabler, when he sent his rented team and buggy back by another person). But the trip proved to

---

140 The running of drafts for Maryland soldiers is mentioned in Helen Jones Campbell, *The Case for Mrs. Surratt* (New York: G. P. Putnam's Sons, 1943), 68, and detailed in full in Howell's manuscript testimony before the military commission trying the Lincoln conspirators, 234-39, included with Howell's records, ancestry.com. In general, see Elizabeth Stegner Trindall, *Mary Surratt: An American Tragedy* (Gretna: Pelican Publishing Co., 1996) 92, 96-98, Campbell, *Case for Mrs. Surratt*, 74; Louis J Weichmann, *A True Story of Abraham Lincoln and of the Conspiracy of 1865* (Edited by Floyd E. Risvold. New York: Alfred A. Knopf, 1975), 85-86, 120-22; George S. Bryan, *The Great American Myth: The True Story of Lincoln's Murder* (Chicago: Americana House, 1990), 237-38, 245.

be too much for the former seminary student as he found Slater to be as tough as any Confederate soldier and a born killer.[141]

Meanwhile, refusing to take an oath of future loyalty to the union, Howell rotted in the Old Capitol until July 8, when he finally yielded to the facts of the Confederacy's demise and the recent execution of the Lincoln co-conspirators and swore to be a good Yankee citizen.[142] He was released the next day. But this was after he was called into face the military commission trying the accused assassins to attest to Mary Surratt's myopia. On the stand, Howell proved to be as slippery as the proverbial eel. He admitted to nothing beyond Mary Surratt's poor eyesight. He did not know his name, or how he got it; was vague about his activities during the war, beyond carrying money to Maryland families of Confederate soldiers a couple of times; and seemed to be incapable of remembering anything else. While completely exasperating the prosecuting and defense attorneys, he probably did Mary Surratt little good as he was arrested at her tavern and was an admitted, although disabled, former Confederate soldier. But behind the scenes he did his best to implicate the turncoat Weichmann, now testifying against his former landlady.[143]

---

141 The arrest is detailed in various document copies from Microfilm M-374, Reel 194, National Archives and Records Administration, Unfiled Papers and Slips Belonging in Compiled Confederate Service Records, in Augustus Howell file, James O. Hall papers, JOHRC. For Surratt's eye opener on Slater, see William L. Richter, *Confederate Freedom Fighter: The Story of John H. Surratt & the Plots against Lincoln* (Laurel, Md.: Burgundy, 2007), 146 (women on the brain), 147-52.

142 Tidwell papers, drawer # 8, JOHRC.

143 Howell's manuscript testimony before the military commission trying the Lincoln conspirators, *passim*, included with Howell's records, ancestry.com. See also, Larson, *Assassin's Accomplice*, 164-67; Kauffman, *American Brutus*, 357-58, 361-62, for Howell's testimony probably harming Mrs. Surratt than helping her. On Howell's attempt to implicate Weichmann, see H. Donald Winkler's, *Lincoln and Booth: More Light on the Conspiracy* (Nashville: Cumberland House, 2003), 223. Also of interest, Thomas R. Turner, "Did Weichmann Turn State's Evidence to Save Himself?" *Lincoln Herald*, 81 (Winter 1979), 265-67; and Joseph George Jr., "Nature's First Law: Louis J. Weichmann and Mrs. Surratt," *Civil War History*, 28 (1982), 101-27, especially 111-12. Weichmann, who got out of his predicament by singing like a controlled songbird, as the Federals demanded, has had his statements against Howell preserved in William C. Edwards and Edward Steers, Jr., *The Lincoln Assassination: The Evidence* [a print version of the Lincoln Assassination Suspects file on Microfilm M-599, 12

After his release from the Old Capitol Prison, Howell disappeared into the shadows once again. It is not known how he occupied himself for the few brief years that remained to his life, or where exactly that he resided. It is known that he had relatives living near the Navy Yard and it is possible that he may have spent time with them, but this is not known for certain. This lack of information is certainly in keeping with Howell's elusive and mysterious wartime career and is indicative of his efficiency and effectiveness in his capacity as an agent of the Confederacy. Far from "smarmy" and "arrogant," as characterized by a recent historian, or a murderer as falsely accused by contemporaries, surely "secretive, elusive and effective" were the characteristics of Howell and most men and women like him who served between and behind the lines during the war.[144]

In 1869, Augustus Howell would suffer a final bout of typhoid fever to which he would succumb. Howell's death notice, or obituary, which appeared in the December 24, 1869, edition of *The Prince Georgian*, in column 2 of page 2, reads as follows: "Died, in Washington, on Friday, the 10th instant, Augustus Howell, formerly of Charles, but for the last ten years a citizen of this county." He was interred at Congressional Cemetery in Washington, D.C. on December 12, 1869. The cause of death cited on his burial certificate was "bilious typhus," his old Civil War ailment.[145]

Rolls, National Archives and Records Administration] (Urbanna: University of Illinois Press, 2009), 1318, 1324, 1327, 1329. See also Larson, *Assassin's Accomplice*, 186.

144 Larson, *Assassin's Accomplice*, 58 (smarmy and arrogant); discussion at Lincoln-Assassination.com, Discussions, All Things Lincoln Assassination, topic: Augustus Howell and Emack (accused murderer); and Gaddy, "Confederate Spy Unmasked: An Afterward," 94 (secret, elusive, and effective).

145 See death notice and burial in Congressional Cemetery, with documents in ancestry. com. See also, communication of James O. Hall to Custodian, Congressional Cemetery, January 10, 1869, listing plot number, drawer #8, Tidwell papers, JOHRC.

V.

ISAAC IN TEXAS

A Theoretical Look at the Other Surratt

Everyone interested in the assassination of President Abraham Lincoln is aware of the woman in the story, Mary E. Surratt, who was hanged for her part in the conspiracy. Through her, most are cognizant of her younger son, John H. Surratt, Jr., who fled to Europe after the assassination, later to be hauled back in chains and tried for the same crime, ultimately to be set free because of a deadlocked jury. Others are familiar with Mary's beautiful, raven-haired daughter, Anna, who grieved at her mother's death. Fewer still know much of John Surratt, Sr., Mary's besotted husband and ne'er-do-well barkeep, struck down by apoplexy in 1862. But not many are acquainted with Mary's eldest son, Isaac; some having a vague idea that he lived out the war in Texas, serving as a mail rider and was a member of an obscure regiment in the Confederate Army. This essay is an attempt to surmise what Isaac's wartime experiences were like, using available information to fill out his largely undocumented life in the West.

Isaac Douglas Surratt was born in the District of Columbia on June 2, 1841 and baptized at St. Peter's Roman Catholic Church in Washington three months later. Isaac grew into a handsome young man, about five feet eight inches tall, with blue eyes, thick brown hair and full, imperial-style beard. He was a well-educated but indifferent student, whose mother used her connections with local priests to get him a job as a clerk at a Baltimore mercantile establishment just before the Civil War to keep him from what she saw as the malevolent influence of his alcoholic father. Troubled by the election of Abraham Lincoln and the Republican take-over of Congress upon the secession of the Lower South, Isaac came home on March 4, 1861, the day Lincoln was inaugurated, and announced that he was going to Texas. How he went, by land or sea, is unknown, but GTT (Gone To Texas), as it was called in those days, was a common antebellum solution to any Southerner's personal, social, legal, or political problems.[146]

When Isaac arrived in Texas, he headed for San Antonio, the state's largest city. The idea that Isaac was hoping to ride for the Pony Express in Texas is incorrect as its route went across the northern plains from St. Joseph. Missouri, and it was, in any case, defunct by then. But he could have carried local mail on horseback throughout 1861. Be that as it may, Isaac found San Antonio to be a bustling place, filled with a diverse population divided roughly in three equal parts. There were German immigrants, refugees from the failed 1848 revolutions in Europe who still carried on much of the business of their daily life conversing in the Teutonic tongue and were pro-Union as regarded the war. Then there were native-born Mexicans, called *tejanos*, predominantly Spanish-speakers, who had dominated the region before the Texas Revolution and had been isolated from their homeland since and were politically neutral regarding secession. Finally, there was a diverse group of English-speaking Northern

---

[146] The standard biography of the Surratts is Elizabeth Stegner Trindal, *Mary Surratt*), for Isaac, see 20, 42, 45, 54, 56, 66, 147, 231-32. A shorter, excellent thumbnail sketch is in Larson, *The Assassin's Accomplice*, 11-25, for Isaac, see 12, 21, 25, 29, 227. For further information on Isaac's looks and life, see also, James O. Hall to —?—, June 15, 1854; Margaret Bearden to Dr. Richard Mudd, January 12, 1962; James O. Hall to Laurie Verge, August 29, 1986, all in James O. Hall papers, JOHRC, Surratt House Museum.

Europeans, incorrectly referred to as Anglos, from the rest of the United States, most of whom had arrived since 1836 and who supported the Confederacy.

Newcomer Isaac soon learned that, just as it had been for the United States before secession, San Antonio was now the headquarters of the Confederate Army for all operations to the west toward New Mexico Territory (essentially Indian country filled with roaming bands of hostile Lipan Apaches, Kiowas, and Comanches), and south to the Rio Grande (an area filled with more horses and maverick cattle than people, most of whom were opportunistic bandits from both sides of the international border). In a semi-circle to the north lay the Texas Hill Country, a half dozen or so counties filled with more Germans, who were passionately against the Southern institution of chattel slavery and secession. Indeed, there were even more German settlements between San Antonio and Austin and Houston, but these had been established as early as 1831 and tended to conform to the predominant slaveholding culture of the Deep South.[147]

Of all these groups, Isaac discovered that it was the thousands of recently arrived Germans, the so-called "48ers," who presented the biggest problem for the Rebel authorities. Although it had taken the Texas secessionists much of 1861 to leave the Union, depose anti-secession governor Sam Houston in favor of Lieutenant Governor Richard Clark, and organize a military defense, the close election of Francis R. Lubbock as governor over Clark in late 1861 had put a staunch Confederate in power at last. Flexing his political muscles, Lubbock stopped

---

[147] For the San Antonio Isaac found, see Richard Selcer and Paul Burrier, "What Really Happened on the Nueces River?: James M. Duff, Good Soldier or "The Butcher of Fredericksburg,'" *North & South*, 1 (January 1998), 56-67.; a memoir of a pro-Confederate German is H. W. Graber, *The Life Record of H. W. Graber, a Terry Texas Ranger, 1861-1865* ([Dallas]: H. W. Graber, 1916). In general, see Egon Richard Tausch, "Southern Sentiment among the Texas Germans during the Civil War and Reconstruction" (Unpublished MA Thesis, University of Texas, 1965).

sending state soldiers to the east and began to concentrate on Texas' domestic safety by suppressing indigenous pro-Union factions.[148]

Like Lubbock, Isaac came to realize that the Germans had a history of acting independently on the West Texas frontier. Immediately after settling in the Texas Hill Country they established the Freemen's Association, a political society that tried to keep a neutrality between the pro-Union Germans and the pro-Southern elements. Upon the withdrawal of the U.S. Army from the frontier, the Germans created numerous home guard companies, ostensibly to protect themselves from the Comanches. But since the Germans has signed a separate peace treaty with these "Lords of the Southern Plains" in 1854, leaving the rest of Texas in the lurch, their stated purpose rang hollow to the newly seceded state government.[149]

Worst of all, Isaac learned, the Germans created the first Union Loyal Leagues, the *avant garde* of the Republican party. This action alone cancelled what little good the Freemen's Association had achieved with the burgeoning Confederacy. When Colonel Ben McCulloch and 1500 Texas state troops occupied San Antonio in February 1861 to receive the surrender of the Federal Army on the plains, he soon spoke of the need of martial law to subdue dissidents.

Isaac knew that Colonel McCulloch's fear was driven by the state referendum on secession, which had revealed that around

---

148 A quick sketch of Texas Civil War politics is in William L. Richter, *The Army in Texas during Reconstruction, 1865-1870* (College Station: Texas A & M Press, 1987), 3-8. The dislike of all Texans for any type of military rule, be it Mexican, U.S., or C.S., is discussed in Richter, "'Devil Take Them All': Military Rule in Texas, 1862-1870," *Southern Studies: An Interdisciplinary Journal of the South*, 25 (Spring 1986), 5-30.

149 On the Germans in Texas, see Rudolf Leopold Biesele, *The History of the German Settlements in Texas, 1831-1961* (San Marcos, Tex.: German-Texan Heritage Society, 1987); Terry G. Jordan, *German Seed in Texas Soil: Immigrant Farmers in Nineteenth Century Texas* (Austin: University of Texas Press, 1966); D. W. Meinig, *Imperial Texas: An Interpretive Essay in Cultural Geography* (Austin: University of Texas, 1969); Glen E. Lich, *The German Texans* (San Antonio: University of Texas Institute of Texas Cultures, 1981).

25% of the state was very much opposed leaving the Union. This opposition was located on the northern and western borders of the state, and was especially pronounced in the German Hill Country above San Antonio. Coming from a family of obvious Confederate sympathies, Isaac quickly succumbed to the perceived emergency.[150]

On May 4, 1862, Isaac D. Surratt enrolled with Brigadier General James M. Duff, a Texas state recruiting officer and member of the pro-secession Knights of the Golden Circle, who had raised some of the first militia companies that had accepted the surrender of the U.S. Eighth Infantry and Second Cavalry coming in from the forts on the plains. Isaac joined Captain Richard Taylor's Company A, Texas Partisan Dragoons, as a private. Isaac received a $150 allowance for his horse and $50 for "equipments," which means he brought into the service his own mount, saddle and bridle, pistol, clothes, and a blanket to cover himself with at night. How much clothing in Confederate gray he received is open to conjecture, maybe a jacket and a cap.[151]

Isaac reported for duty three days later to find that General Duff had resigned his Texas state commission to join the Provisional Army of the Confederate States as a captain and field commander of what was now Duff's Texas Partisan Corps or Partisan Rangers, a squadron with two mounted companies, one of which was Taylor's Company A. With three weeks of rudimentary training under their belts, Isaac and the rest of Duff's Partisans headed into the Texas Hill Country on May 28. They were to enforce the First Confederate Conscription Act (April

---

[150] Selcer and Burrier, "What Really Happened on the Nueces River?" 56-59.
[151] Military Record of Isaac D. Surratt, 1862-1865, Microcopy M227, Roll 35, National Archives and Records Service. We wish to thank Archivist Trevor Plante for helping us ascertain the completeness of this record and Tim Mulligan of the Surratt Society for connecting us with Mr. Plante.

16, 1862) and district commander Brigadier General Hamilton Bee's declaration of martial law in the German counties.

By May 30, two days after Isaac and Duff's Partisan Rangers arrived at their destination, Fredericksburg, Gillespie County, overall Rebel state commander Brigadier General Paul O. Hebert placed the entire State of Texas under martial law. The declaration was published in English and German (not Spanish), leaving little doubt as to who was the intended target of the enforcement of Confederate policies. All males over 16 years of age had ten days to report and take an oath of loyalty to the state and the Confederacy or face a jail term and confiscation of property. By June 20, Isaac and his fellow soldiers had signed up most of the male population and arrested three or four of the leaders most hostile to the Southern war effort. Operations extended from Gillespie into Medina, Blanco, Kendall and Kerr counties. Opposition was minimal and non-violent.

Isaac returned to San Antonio with the rest of his Partisan Rangers to attend the meeting of the military commission which was about to try all disloyal parties they had arrested.[152] But as the court convened, reports came in from the German counties of constant pro-Union bushwacking and raids that local authorities could not or would not suppress. By July 21, Isaac and Duff's Partisan Rangers returned to Fredericksburg in response to the murders of two Confederate supporters. This time, Duff ordered that all males come in and retake the oath of allegiance to Texas and the Confederacy within three days or suffer the usual consequences..

Few came in. Isaac and his company divided into twenty-man patrols and received orders to scour the countryside. This

---

152 The trials are documented in Alwyn Barr (ed.), "Records of the Confederate Military Commission in San Antonio, July 20-October 10, 1862," *Southwestern Historical Quarterly*, 70 (1966-67), 93-109, 289-313, 623-44; 71 (1967-68), 247-78.

time they arrested Unionists and their families, seized property, and hauled all suspected Union supporters back into Fredericksburg or old Ft. Mason nearby. The Germans protested that Duff and his men were acting like the very Prussians they had fled Germany to avoid. It was not long before Duff was being called the "Butcher of Fredericksburg," although how many men he hanged or shot and how much property he seized or destroyed is disputed. Whether Isaac felt any remorse for the troops' actions is unrecorded. Certainly some of the Partisan Rangers disliked what they were doing.[153]

Then Isaac and his comrades learned from informers that 65 Germans under the age of 35, or prime military recruits, were fleeing for Mexico intent on joining pro-Union Texas forces organizing in Matamoros at the mouth of the Rio Grande. Duff sent Lieutenant Colin D. Macrae and 94 men, drawn from the Partisan Rangers, the 8th Texas Cavalry, some state militia, and the 2nd Texas Mounted Rifles, in pursuit. On August 10, the Confederates came upon the Germans encamped at the Nueces river and charged into their camp during the early hours before dawn.

The ensuing Battle of the Nueces, or the "Nueces Massacre," as the Germans came to call it, scattered the Union men, killing 28 (most of whom were executed when they surrendered after being wounded), and cost the Rebel cavalry 20 men killed and wounded. Modern historians believe that "battle" is more accurate than "massacre" as both sides were heavily armed and fought with abandon. Whether Isaac was among the troops at the Nueces is unknown—his commander Captain Duff was not. If Isaac were present, it might explain his reticence to speak

---

[153] See, *e.g.*, the memoirs of one of Isaac's fellow soldiers, R. H. Williams, *With the Border Ruffians: Memories of the Far West, 1852-1868* (Lincoln: University of Nebraska press, 1982), 230-35.

of his war experiences. Indeed, the whole of Duff's Partisan Rangers, including Isaac, was back in San Antonio by the end of the month. They would never engage in provost marshal duty again.[154]

By this time, Duff's squadron had been expanded and granted a more formal organization as the 14th Battalion of Texas Cavalry, with Duff receiving quick promotions from captain to major to lieutenant colonel. Duff's second in command was Major James R. Sweet, his former San Antonio business partner. Isaac Surratt went with Captain Taylor's Company A to Ft. Esperanza near Victoria to guard the Gulf coast against Yankee invasion. After the three or four new companies were organized in San Antonio, Isaac's company rejoined the full battalion, which was ordered to the Lower Rio Grande Valley, where it spent the rest of 1862 and all of 1863 awaiting the Union onslaught and chasing Mexican bandits. It was here that Isaac wrote his only letter home and fed his mother the mail rider story to quash her fears for his safety.[155]

By the fall of 1863, Duff's 14th Texas Cavalry Battalion received several more companies of recruits and was reorganized as the 33rd Texas Cavalry Regiment or Partisan Rangers, with a second major, Santos Benavides, reflecting the Hispanic nature of newer recruits. In late October and early November of 1863, Union troops landed at Brazos Santiago at the mouth of the Rio Grande and advanced upstream on Brownsville to seal off the cross-border trade between the Confederacy and Maximillian's French and Austrians in Mexico.

Isaac and the men of Company A scouted the Union

---

154 On the occupation of the Hill Country, martial law, and the Battle of the Nueces, see Selcer and Burrier, "What Really Happened on the Nueces River?" 59-67; Robert W. Shook, "The Battle of the Nueces, August 10, 1862," *Southwestern Historical Quarterly*, 66 (1962-63), 31-62; Stanley S. McGowen, "Battle or Massacre? The Incident on the Nueces, August 10, 1862," *ibid.*, 104 (2000-2001), 65-86; Frank W. Heintzen, "Fredericksburg, Texas, in Civil War and Reconstruction" (Unpublished MA Thesis, St. Mary's University [San Antonio], 1944).

155 Stewart Sifakis, *Compendium of the Confederate Armies: Texas* (New York: Facts on File, 1995), 70, 90. Unfortunately, of merely marginal value is John Rigdon, *Historical Sketch & Roster [of] the Texas 33rd Cavalry Regiment* (Clearwater, S.C.: Eastern Digital Resources, 2007).

approach but were driven off as they covered the Confederate withdrawal to Santa Gertrudis (present-day Kingsville). Two of Company A's soldiers were killed when Captain Adrian Vidal and a whole company of six-months enlistees deserted to the Union cause. Isaac Surratt may nor may not have been one of the regiment's nineteen wounded in these frays but, in December 1863, he spent two weeks in the military hospital at Victoria for an unlisted cause.[156]

Restored to good health, Isaac Surratt and the 33rd Texas Cavalry passed through most of 1864 stationed near Victoria, Indianola, and Ft. Esperanza, except for a journey up north to Bonham during the Federal Army's failed campaign on Camden, Arkansas, in conjunction with another abortive Union drive up the Red River. Back in the Lower Rio Grande Valley by that fall, Company A and Isaac Surratt, now a sergeant and acting quartermaster, fought a skirmish at Palmito (often incorrectly spelled "Palmetto") Hill on September 6. 1864, that resulted from Company A's attempt to herd a *remuda* of horses destined for remounts past Union positions. This foray is often confused with the real battle fought there May 12 and 13, 1865, known the last battle of the Civil War (a Confederate victory, by the way), in which the Partisan Rangers took no part.[157]

On May 25, 1865, recognizing the inevitable, the Confederate Commander of the Trans-Mississippi Department, Major General Edmund Kirby Smith, surrendered all Rebel troops west of the Father of Waters. But many of the troops in Texas, especially those from Arkansas and Missouri, simply went home

---

156 The role of Surratt's company is detailed in Frank C. Pierson, *A Brief History of the Lower Rio Grande Valley* (Menasha, Wisc.: George Bamta Publishing Company, 1917), 42-43. See also Military Record of Isaac D. Surratt, 1862-1865, Microcopy M227, Roll 35, National Archives and Records Service. Of general interest is Jerry Don Thompson, *Vaqueros in Blue and Gray* (Austin: State House Press, 2000).

157 Pierson, *A Brief History of the Lower Rio Grande Valley*, 50. Erroneous listings of the 33rd Texas Cavalry being at Palmito as the last battle of the Civil War include Sifakis, *Compendium*, 90, Trindal, *Mary Surratt*, 231. For Isaac's promotion, see Military Record of Isaac D. Surratt, 1862-1865, Microcopy M227, Roll 35, National Archives and Records Service.

without formally surrendering, in an unofficial movement called the "break-up." Isaac Surratt may have been a part of the break-up. Indeed, he never signed a parole until September 18, 1865, giving some substance to the notion that he and his companions crossed the Rio Grande and joined up with Maximillian's forces, as did thousands of other of Americans. But when the French officers refused to allow Surratt and his fellows to elect their own officers, the Americans returned to Texas and took the oath of future loyalty to the Union in front of the provost marshal at San Antonio.[158]

It was at this time that Surratt allegedly received a purse from his comrades to finance his way east to assassinate President Andrew Johnson as revenge for the execution of his mother. Warned by Major General Philip Sheridan, now U.S. commander in Texas, Brigadier General Lafayette C. Baker's National Detective Police watched and reported on Isaac when he arrived in Baltimore, but never arrested him. He went to work for the Old Bay Line shipping company as an auditor, ultimately under the tutelage of his brother, John. Isaac was a quiet man who never married, but remained content to live out the remainder of his life with his sister Anna and her husband, chemist William Tonry in the Monument City, until his death in 1907. To the end, he would always remain, "the other Surratt."[159]

---

158 The statement of James O. Hall (James O. Hall to Laurie Verge, August 29, 1986, James O. Hall papers, JOHRC Surratt House Museum) that he could not understand why Surratt and his comrades would fight for Maximillian is contradicted by history. See, e.g., Edwin Adams Davis, *Fallen Guidon: The Forgotten Saga of General Jo Shelby's Confederate Command*... (Santa Fe: Stagecoach Press, 1962).

159 Trindal, *Mary Surratt*, 231-33; Military Record of Isaac D. Surratt, 1862-1865, Microcopy M227, Roll 35, National Archives and Records Service. See also, James O. Hall to —?—, June 15, 1854; Margaret Bearden to Dr. Richard Mudd, January 12, 1962; James O. Hall to Laurie Verge, August 29, 1986 all in James O. Hall papers, JOHRC, Surratt House Museum.

VI.

"I DON'T REALLY KNOW WHAT TO MAKE OF IT"

The Owens Statement, the Survival of Booth's Horses, and the Move to the Potomac

Even now, 150 years after Abraham Lincoln's assassination, the story of the escape of his assailant, John Wilkes Booth, has many inconvenient holes in it that puzzle the honest reader and interrupt the thread of the established tale. One of these incongruities is the Owens statement, the testimony cruelly extracted[160] from James Owens[161] by Colonel Henry H. Wells behind the often too porous walls of the Bryantown Tavern, Union army headquarters during much if the pursuit of Booth and David E. Herold, his erstwhile companion, on their road south.

It was obvious that Owens, a young black employee in Austin L. Adams' Tavern at Newport, Maryland, and one of Wells' more brutalized witnesses (he would die from his mal-

---

160 There few verbs that can describe what psychological and physical brutalities Wells did to suspected accomplices and reluctant witnesses alike. Foe another, see fn. 9, below. His subordinates did much the same. See Thomas Jones, Thomas A. Jones, *John Wilkes Booth: An Account of His Sojourn through Southern Maryland* (Chicago: Laird & Lee, 1893), 122, who said of Wells, "a rougher man I have never had to deal with." For more on Jones, see John M. and Roberta J. Wearmouth, *Thomas A. Jones: Chief Agent of the Confederate Secret Service in Maryland*... (Port Tobacco, MD.: Stone's Throw Publishing, 2000).

161 Owens was described by one Federal officer as "an ignorant, stubborn fellow, [who] will require the sternest measures to elicit anything from him." See William C. Edwards and Edward Steers, Jr., *The Lincoln Assassination: The Evidence* (Urbana: University of Illinois Press, 2009), 353.

treatment in the prison hospital, June 22, 1865), "had a heck of a lot of information about a lot of things," admitted premier Booth escape historian James O. Hall, "but I don't really know what to make of it."[162] Evidently, neither do other historians, as they conveniently overlook the Owens statement and its full implications in their neat, accepted narratives.[163]

But not all historians are so remiss. J. E. "Rick" Smith, III, a sometime docent at the Surratt House Museum in Clinton, Maryland, and investigator of the Booth escape ride, is one who doubts the accepted narrative. In a series of contributions to the Surratt Society's monthly newsletter, he suggests a solution to James O. Hall's puzzlement by making something of "it"—the Owens statement, the key role of the Adams' Newport Tavern, and the fate of Booth and Herold's equine accomplices.[164]

---

162 See Hall's comments on the Owens Statement, in James O. Hall to Joan Chaconas, n.d., courtesy of Joan Chaconas. The Owens Statement without Hall's comments is also in the James Owens filea, William A. Tidwell papers, JOHRC. For the date of Owens' death, see Tidwell's comments, A. L. Adams file, *ibid*. The Adamses were arrested at the same time as Owens in April and released on June 25, 1865.

163 See, e.g., Lloyd Lewis, *The Assassination of Lincoln: History and Myth* (New York: Harcourt, Brace and Company, 1929); George S. Bryan, *The Great American Myth: The True Story of Lincoln's Murder* (New York: Carrick &, Evans, 1940); William Hanchett, *The Lincoln Murder Conspiracies* . . . (Urbana: University of Illinois Press, 1983); Jay Winik, *April 1865: The Month that Saved America* (New York: HarperCollins, 2001); H. Donald Winkler, *Lincoln and Booth: More Light on the Conspiracy* (Nashville, Tn.: Cumberland House, 2003); Kauffman, *American*; Swanson, *Manhunt*; Bill O'Reilly and Martin Dugard, *Killing Lincoln: The Shocking Assassination that Changed America Forever* (New York: Henry Holt and Company, 2011), all ignore the Owns Statement.

   William A Tidwell, James O. Hall, and David W. Gaddy, *Come Retribution: The Confederate Secret Service and the Assassination of Lincoln* (Jackson: University Press of Mississippi, 1988), 431-32, mention the Owens Statement but only as regards its mention of the rowing of Confederate spies Thomas Harbin and Joseph Baden across the Potomac, but not its reference to Booth and Herold, as does Edward Steers, Jr., in *Blood on the Moon: The Assassination of Abraham Lincoln* (Lexington: University of Kentucky Press, 2001), 194, 322, and his *The Lincoln Assassination Encyclopedia* (HarperCollins, 2010), 3, 416-17.

   Edwards and Steers, *The Lincoln Assassination: The Evidence*, 551-53, especially 552; and 1375-77, especially 1376, which are lists of prisoners at the Old Capitol Prison that mention Mr. and Mrs. Austin L. Adams and James Owens as arrested by order of Col Wells for aiding Booth to escape. The authors in their footnotes (p. 1376) dispute this fact and the prison commandant William P. Wood recommended that they be released, partially because of age (he was 64 and she was "over 50"). See Wood's statement on p. 1375.

164 See J. E. "Rick" Smith, III, "The Owens Statement," *Surratt Courier*, 32 (No. 10, October 2007), 3-6; "What Is Horse-Faking?" *ibid.*, 33 (No. 4, April 2008), 4-6; "More on the Fate of the Horses," *ibid.*, 33 (No. 5, May 2008), 4-5.

If one goes to Newport today, there are still a few isolated buildings, but no remnants of what might have been Adams' Tavern. Locals say a "drinking place" and a post office once existed at the northwest corner of the confluence of Allen's Fresh and Newport turnpikes with the road to Bryantown leading to the north. Smith envisions what might have been: a two-story structure of the typical American balloon frame construction so popular in the last two centuries, and so common to Southern Maryland before and after the Civil War, with a steeply pitched roof, sheathed with split cedar shakes; clapboard siding, in this particular case painted a very light shade of yellow; tall windows, with dark green shutters thrown open and facing to every point of the compass; narrow, red brick chimneys standing at each of its two gable ends; long, narrow, raised porch running the length of its south facing elevation, with steps at the right end; and hanging from the porch, over the stair, a signboard which read, "Adams House Tavern, Austin Adams, Prop."[165]

All reverie aside, the historical record on James Owens began on April 28, 1865, a couple of days after John Wilkes Booth died at Richard Garret's Locust Hill farm just south of the Rappahannock River in Virginia. Jailed at the Bryantown Tavern along with Austin and Adeline Adams and others, Owens reluctantly gave his story to Colonel Henry H. Wells, after he was "handcuffed and hung up," as stated in Colonel Welles' report. It is a bit confused, as Owens skipped around in his coerced "confession," but once the dates are straightened out, a very interesting tale emerges.

Owens commenced by saying that the whole episode began two weeks prior, with the arrival of two men at the Newport tavern, which seemingly makes no sense as Booth had yet to

---

165 Smith, "The Adams Tavern, Newport, Maryland," *ibid.*, 38 (No. 10, October 2013), 11-13.

shoot the president. But what Owens was actually referring to is the arrival of three men on April 15, before any of those at Newport had heard of the Lincoln shooting.[166] These men were Confederate agent Thomas Harbin, his telegraphic assistant, Private Joseph Baden, and Lieutenant W. Garland Smith of Colonel John Mosby's Company G. These men were on a weeklong mission to extract and escort back to Virginia an explosives team led by Sergeant Thomas F. Harney that had been sent to blow up the White House and its occupants; an escaped Confederate spy, Lieutenant B. Frank Stringfellow; and Lincoln's assassin, John Wilkes Booth and whoever might accompany him.

Instead of linking up with any of the expected Confederates, Smith's cavalry platoon clashed with a Union mounted patrol at Mechanicsville, north of Newport. In the confusion of the after-dark skirmish, the Confederates retreated to Newport, uncertain how many Yankees they had confronted. There, Harbin and Smith decided to scatter the Rebel command to their homes (most of them were from Southern Maryland and Robert E. Lee's Army of Northern Virginia had long since surrendered) and cross the Potomac with Baden to their Virginia headquarters.[167]

Their boatman would be Owens, who received five dollars for the trip, which interrupted Owens' fishing for shad with gill nets. Owens at first maintained that he crossed the three men over a "run" at Allen's Fresh on the way to Banks o' Dee. But under later questioning by Lieutenant S. P. Currier at the Old Capitol Prison in Washington City, the officer, in the words of one historian, "wrung out" of Owens an admission that the

---

166 Testimony of George D. Allory, May 15, 1865, Edwards and Steers, *The Lincoln Assassination: The Evidence*, 8-9. Allory was a neighbor of the Adamses.
167 William A. Tidwell, "April 15, 1865," *Surratt Courier*, 22 (April-May-June 1997), 6-10, 5-10, 4-9.

boatman took them all the way across to Mathias Point in Virginia.[168]

This much of the Owens statement historians seem to agree on. They point out that Harbin's party, which Owens rowed across the Potomac, was mistakenly assumed to contain Booth and Herold, when reported to pursuing Federal provost marshals. This incorrect surmise became the critical piece of information that accidentally set Union Colonel Lafayette C. Baker's detectives and their cavalry escort into the Northern Neck and ultimately across the Rappahannock River to Garrett's Farm and Booth's final reckoning.[169]

But the rest of Owen's story is a potential gold mine of new information on Booth's escape from Maryland. Although, Owens denied ever seeing Stringfellow, he remembered that at suppertime on Thursday night, April 20, two bedraggled white men had showed up at the tavern, "accompanied by a white boy." He recollected their horses, too. One was "a roan or iron-gray, and the other was a light bay with a small star on the forehead."

One of the riders Owens described was "lame and carried a crutch; he wore a cloth slipper on his right foot, and carried the crutch under his right arm. He had on a close-bodied coat and wore a shawl; he was a stouter man than the other," continued Owens, "who was a small man, I think that he had very light whiskers; he wore two coats and a soft, black, low-crowned hat with a narrow brim." Owens had just described John Wilkes Booth and David E. Herold and their stolen Washington City livery horses to a Tee.

The "white boy," was most likely Samuel Cox, Jr. Although

---

[168] "Wrung out" is in a hand-written comment by William A. Tidwell in A. L. Adams File, Tidwell papers, JOHRC. See also, Tidwell, Hall, and Gaddy, *Come Retribution*, 431-32; Edwards and Steers, Jr., *The Lincoln Assassination: The Evidence*, 409 (where Currier erroneously refers to James Owens as George Henry Owens); Steers, *The Lincoln Assassination Encyclopedia*, 3, 416-17.

[169] Tidwell, Hall, and Gaddy, *Come Retribution*, 468-69.

Owens said nothing to the Federal inquisitors about it, Booth and Herold had just spent several days camped out in the woods south and west of Rich Hill, the plantation owned by Cox's stepfather, a spot located about seven miles west of Newport.

Tavern keeper Adams was momentarily absent when the three riders arrived, but he came in about thirty minutes later. Owens had chores to do but as he left the tavern he briefly heard the riders conversing with Adams and his wife out front. The lame man (Booth) asked Adams if there "were any Yankees or soldiers around." The barkeep replied, "There had been none for two or three months." "How far were they from the Potomac?" queried Booth. Adams answered, "About six miles." Mrs. Adams then stated that the strangers could not stay at Newport, as she was afraid that Union soldiers would come and catch them. But, she ventured, "I will give y'all something to eat."

After they ate, Adams directed the travelers to a copse of woods west across the road. They stayed in the pines overnight and most of the next day, occasionally coming up to the tavern to eat, drink, and pass the time of day. After dark, Booth and Herold, guided by the "white boy" (again, probably young Cox) and the newly arrived Thomas Jones on his old nag, Kit, rode off toward the west. Jones rode out ahead to scout their way and avoid possible Union troopers. Owen heard Mrs. Adams ask where the men were going and they said Pope's Creek, where Jones lived.

The next day, young Sam Cox came back with the two horses used by Booth and Herold. He said that Jones had got the two fugitives across the Potomac. As to the fate of the horses, Owens opined, "[i]f I were to try to find them I would inquire of the people there who saw them." Owens then proceeded to name a half dozen nearby residents who might have seen the men at Adams' place or riding by at night toward Pope's Creek. But by the time the pursuers of Booth and Herold heard this, Booth was dead and Herold on his way to a military trial and hanging. None of those named by Owens as possibly seeing the Booth cavalcade was ever arrested.[170]

Booth and Herold's horses were never seen again.[171] But then, the two steeds were supposed to have already been dead for several days when they showed up at Adams' Tavern on April 20. At least according to Thomas Jones, Colonel Prentiss Ingraham and Lieutenant Mortimer B. Ruggles.

Jones said that he had found Booth's horse loose and grazing near their campsite in the pines west of Rich Hill. He cautioned Booth about this, saying that a loose horse would tip off any federal patrol to search the area further. So, Jones, Herold and/or Cox's overseer, Frank Robey (pick your favorite suspect[s]) took the animals deep into the Zechiah Swamp, shot them with Herold's .52 cal. Spencer carbine, and sunk them in a bog. It was awfully noisy business for men who were not trying to attract attention.[172]

Prentiss and Ruggles told a different story. In a turn-of-the-century article in *Century Magazine*, they said that when Booth and Herold set off into the Potomac they pulled the horses into the river after them and slit their throats. The steeds floated off in the tide and sank out of sight never to be seen again. But dead bodies in water have an unfortunate propensity to bloat and float and be seen by passersby like constant patrolling Union naval personnel.[173]

---

170 Owens Statement, in James Owens File, William A. Tidwell papers, JOHRC.

171 See Col. Wells report to Maj. Gen. C. C. Augur, April 26, 1865, in Edwards and Steers, *The Lincoln Assassination: The Evidence*, 1347.

172 See Smith, "What Is Horse-Faking?" *ibid.*, 33 (No. 4, April 2008), 4-6; "More on the Fate of the Horses," *ibid.*, 33 (No. 5, May 2008), 4-5; Jones, *John Wilkes Booth*, 80-81.

173 See Smith, "What Is Horse-Faking?" *ibid.*, 33 (No. 4, April 2008), 4-6; "More on the Fate of the Horses," *ibid.*, 33 (No. 5, May 2008), 4-5; Prentiss Ingraham, " Pursuit and Death

Owens, however, had described the two horses with an uncanny exactitude on April 28 and said they had returned to Newport in the hands of young Cox on April 23, days after their reputed execution. The solution to this conundrum is actually explained by A. Conan Doyle's detective hero, Sherlock Holmes, says historian Rick Smith. In the mystery "Silver Blaze," Holmes finds a lost racehorse that had been altered in appearance with dye and shoe polish by the artistic skills of a horse-faker.[174] The author of the Civil War history of the First Massachusetts Cavalry agreed with Doyle unwittingly, when he admitted that he and his fellow troopers constantly used such color-altering skills and a liberal use of scissors from men in their own ranks to conceal the identity of horses that they had "liberated" from their Southern masters with great effect.[175]

Why is Owens' testimony left out of the Booth escape story? Probably because the Owens Statement does not fit in with Thomas Jones' memoirs released at the turn-of-the-century. Jones was a clever prevaricator, known throughout Southern Maryland for his unassuming appearance and plausible but suspect stories he fed to his Yankee jailers during the war. His memoirs were designed to reveal his part in the Booth story but to bring harm to his friends and neighbors. He seems to have done a better job than he had hoped. History has bought his mostly spurious tale ever since.

The problem between the Owens Statement and modern historians is that Booth and Herold showed up at the wrong place, at the wrong time, and with the wrong horses. Instead

---

of John Wilkes Booth," *Century Magazine*, 35 (January 1890), 443-48 at 446.

174 William S. Baring-Gould (ed.), *The Annotated Sherlock Holmes* (2 vols., New York: Clarkson N Potter, Inc., Publisher, 1967), II, 261-81.

175 Benjamin W. Crowninshield, *A History of the First Regiment of Massachusetts Cavalry Volunteers* (Boston: Houghton Mifflin, 1891), 291-92. An old family story from the present-day relations of the William Queen family holds that Booth' and Herold's horses spent fruitful lives on the Queen plantation.

of the sandy clearing in the pines and swamps a little south and west of Cox's Rich Hill where, Jones said, their horses had been shot and disposed of days before, here they were, ill-kempt but, with the exception of Booth's broken leg, basically physically sound and well-mounted, and escorted by Cox's step-son. Thomas Jones' published tale has hoodwinked historians ever since.

Why has no one looked beyond Jones' memoirs into Owens' testimony? Why had those who had looked into it merely shrugged their shoulders and dismissed it with reference to James O. Hall's plaintive "I don't really know what to make of it?" An answer might lie in another similar problem that occurred among historians of Reconstruction of Louisiana.

In 1945, noted political and military historian T. Harry Williams of Louisiana State University published his seminal article, "The Louisiana Unification Movement of 1873."[176] The Louisiana Unifiers were a league of rich plantation- and business-oriented whites who had become disgusted with the excesses of the Carpetbag governments that had dominated state politics from the 1862 Union occupation onward. But these men were a relatively small political entity. They needed votes.

One of the larger bloc of voters in Louisiana were the recently freed and enfranchised blacks. The upper class whites had little to fear from integration and social contact with ex-slaves. They had been slave owners, and knew that blacks would never challenge them, economically, politically, or socially. Besides, they "knew" how to "manage" blacks from slavery days. So they offered blacks a deal. They promised them civil rights if the blacks would join them in lowering taxes.

But the Unifiers reckoned without Democrat and Republican politicians, whom the Unifiers threatened to cut out of

---

176 *Journal of Southern History*, 11 (1945), 349-69.

power. Using race as a wedge tactic, the movement failed, when, as the politicians of both parties expected, the mass of poor and middle class whites refused to compromise on economic, and personal, social issues. Indeed, the farther one went from New Orleans, the less inclined the local whites and blacks were to compromise.[177]

This movement was the talk of New Orleans and other newspapers for weeks. Yet before Williams, only one Louisiana historian had even mentioned its existence, albeit briefly.[178] So, at an historical conference Williams got to talking with the premier historian of Louisiana Reconstruction at the time, Ella Lonn, and, when she praised his work, he asked her (she was an excellent researcher) if she had not seen those same newspaper stories. She replied yes, she had. Williams then asked her why she never mentioned them in her book.[179] A puzzled Professor Lonn paused and then said, "I don't know." In her bewilderment, one can hear the echo of James O. Hall's, "I don't really know what to make of it."

But Williams knew. He maintained that such a unification of rich whites and by-and-large poor blacks was not normal in the rest of the South, so Lonn ignored it without even thinking about it. In effect she passed over it without seeing it. It did not fit the accepted story of Reconstruction.[180]

Like Williams, Fawn M. Brodie, controversial biographer of Mormon founder Joseph Smith, Republican Civil War and

---

177 T. Harry Williams, *Romance and Realism in Southern Politics* (Athens: University of Georgia Press, 1961), 17-43, especially 22-23, 29-30, 40-43.

178 Alcee Fortier, *A History of Louisiana* (4 vols., New York: Manzi, Joyant and Company, 1904), IV, part 2, pp. 134-35.

179 Ella Lonn, *Reconstruction in Louisiana After 1868* (New York: G. P. Putnam's Sons, 1918).

180 Williams, *Romance and Realism in Southern Politics*, 19. William wrote this into his book in a general manner, leaving out names. We have added them as he argued it in a Reconstruction class discussion in 1968.

Reconstruction leader Thaddeus Stevens, and President Thomas Jefferson (whom she openly accused of miscegenation with his slave Sally Hemmings), wrote how she made the most in her research of "hitherto unused material," what "in good part ... has been passed over, or ignored because it did not fit into the traditional notions and preconceptions" of the subjects of her studies. Brodie's depiction of Joseph Smith as a fraudulent "genius of improvisation," led to the Latter Day Saints Church excommunication of Brodie in May 1946. She never tried to regain her membership.[181]

In the same manner as with Williams' and Brodie's studies, historians of the Booth escape have ignored the testimony Owens gave. After all, "historians and biographers ... refuse to believe the evidence only because they do not want to," charged Brodie.[182] Booth was where the tradition said he should not be. It did not fit the accepted story and, by the time it surfaced, Booth was dead. Besides the deponent was black and, in those days, in most states he could not even testify before a jury on a case involving white people.

---

181 Fawn M. Brodie, *Thaddeus Stevens: Scourge of the South* (New York: Norton, 1966), 10 (hitherto); *Thomas Jefferson: An Intimate Biography* (New York: Bantam, 1975), xii (in good part); *No Man Knows My Story: The Life of Joseph Smith* (New York: Vintage, 1995), 403 (genius).

182 Brodie, *Thomas Jefferson*, 13, 15; T. Harry Williams, aside to collected students, 1968.

VII.

"I Told Him He Must Go Away"

Elizabeth Rousby Quesenberry and the Escape of Lincoln's Assassin

Today it is a marina. One hundred and forty three years ago it was "The Cottage"; the slowly decaying plantation home of the widow Elizabeth Rose Quesenberry. Located King George County in Virginia's Northern Neck on the banks of Machodac Creek where it joins Williams Creek and empties into the mighty Potomac, most of the Cottage's plantation fields today are within the secured boundaries of the U.S. Navy's Dahlgren Surface Weapons Center.

A century and a half ago, the Cottage's once rich fields lay fallow, most of its slaves gone to digging trenches around Petersburg or runaway to the Promised Land of Freedom up North.[183] But the Cottage was a strategic location on the Confederate States of America's quasi-secret line of communication halfway between Richmond and Washington. The pathway was called the "Doctors' Line," because many of its travelers were supposedly medical men, who hid the letters they carried under the remedies in their medical bags.[184]

---

183 Slaves owned by the Quesenberrys are listed in the 1850 (13 for Mrs. Quesenberry and 18 for her husband) and 1860 (18 for Mr. Quesenberry alone) U.S. Mss Census, available from Ancestry.Com.

184 William A. Tidwell, James O. Hall, & David W. Gaddy, *Come Retribution: The Confederate Secret Service and the Assassination of Lincoln* (Oxford: University Press of Mississippi, 1988), 11, 87-90, 95, 96, 98, 160.

The Cottage was a key station for Rebel secret service agents (most of whom, contrary to legend, were not doctors), who kept a headquarters camp nearby throughout the War for Southern Independence, as they supervised the movement of information and agents between North and South. This line of Communication provided Rebel General Robert E. Lee the means by which to read all of his opponents' military plans blabbed to big city Yankee newspapers a day or two after their publication. Visited often by Union Marine and Navy patrols (it was a semi-secret smuggling route, after all), the house was rumored to have more secret panels and closets than the French Royal Palace at Versailles.[185]

Raised as "Rose" Green, Mrs. Quesenberry (she pronounced it "Quee-zen-berry," but most of her neighbors said "Cue-zen-berry") grew up in the District of Columbia as one of several children of John and Nancy Forrest Green. Her father, whose own father had whose own father had been a privateer and had been lost at sea during the Revolution, worked for the U.S. Department of the Navy. Her mother came from a line of established Georgetown aristocracy, the Rousbys, on one side, and the Platers, on the other. Roses' paternal and maternal grandfathers were Revolutionary War heroes and Jeffersonian politicians.[186]

Born in October 23, 1823, Rose grew up at the family mansion, Rosedale, located between Georgetown and Tenallytown. Her sisters married well; Alice to the heir of the Mexican royal family of Iturbide, Imogene to an established Virginian,

---

[185] Notes by William L. Richter from oral presentation of Michael K. Kauffman, John Wilkes Booth Escape Tour, April 15, 2000.

[186] The only published source to make sense out of the complicated lineage of the Quesenberrys is the fine volume by John Stewart, *Confederate Spies at Large: The Lives of Lincoln Assassination Conspirator and Charlie Russell* (Jefferson, N.C.: McFarland & Company, Inc., Publishers, 2007), 114-116. Other versions are in George H. S. King to James O. Hall, July 19, 1971; James O. Hall to [John] Stanton, January 30, 1985; in JOH Library, Surratt House Museum.

Fielding Lewis. Rose, at the near-spinsterish (in those days) age of 25, finally married widower Nicholas Austin Quesenberry on May 15, 1846. He was from a well-known family that first arrived in Virginia in 1624.[187] He was ten years older than Rose, with a seven year-old daughter and nine year-old son (who would die shortly) by his first wife, who had died herself after giving birth to the daughter.

In the decade that followed heir marriage, Rose gave birth to seven children, three of whom died before reaching age one. But by the time of her husband's natural death in 1863, she was raising four healthy children of her own (two boys and two girls), plus a not-so-happy step daughter, anxious about her share of the property. Ultimately, Mary Louisa would sue step-mother Rose and the case would be settled out of court, each child of each marriage receiving an equal share. Afterward, Rose moved to Texas where she lived in Galveston with three of her surviving children until her death (one daughter had died in the meantime) in 1896. Her death certificate cites "senile decay" as the cause of her demise. Her body was returned home to the District and buried at Holy Rood Cemetery on Wisconsin Avenue N.W.[188]

Throughout her reign as the gracious hostess of the Cottage, Rose Quesenberry, was usually the epitome of proper Southern hospitality, even to visiting Yankees, armed to the teeth, looking for trouble. But by 1865, she was cognizant that her indulgence in allowing Confederate agents access to her property was

---

187 The 1624 date is from Stewart, *Confederate Spies at Large*, 115. Family legend has the Quesenberrys arriving in 1608, bringing the first permanent female settlers to the New World since the abortive settlement at Roanoke Island in the 1680s. See James Nicholas Payne, Notes on Elizabeth Rousby Quesenberry," June 12, 1988, p. 5, copy in Quesenberry File, JOH Library, Surratt House Museum.

188 The court case is summarized in an easily understandable fashion in Stewart, *Confederate Spies at Large*, 127. A fuller exposition is in Payne, "Notes on Elizabeth Rousby Quesenberry," 2-3. The death certificate is in the Quesenbury File, JOH Library, Surratt House Museum.

becoming a liability that might threaten her future freedom and her children's very livelihood.[189]

Whether she was aware of President Abraham Lincoln's assassination ten days earlier (historians think so, family members not), Mrs. Quesenberry was puzzled, if not dismayed, when one of her slaves came up to her at a neighbor's house on the afternoon of April 23, 1865, and informed her that a male stranger, about twenty years old or so, who had just crossed the Potomac from Maryland, had called for her at the Cottage.[190]

When Mrs. Quesenberry arrived back at the Cottage, she found the stranger, who had been bragging to her stepdaughter Louisa[191] of his prowess as an oarsman in crossing the Potomac in a small boat or canoe the night before, had nodded off while sitting against a porch post. Her children's governess, Julia Y. Duncanson, had already fetched up two Confederate agents, one a civilian operative, Thomas H. Harbin, and the other a Con-

---

189 The family's mixed feelings are described in Payne, "Notes on Elizabeth Rousby Quesenberry," 4. Historians have had the benefit of the statement of the Statement of Elizabeth Rousby Quesenberry given to Union Provost Marshal Colonel H. H. Wells, May 16, 1865, Lincoln Assassination Suspects File, Microcopy No. 599, Reel 5, Frames 0556-0559, National Archives and Records Service, reproduced in James O. Hall, *On the Way to Garrett's Farm: John Wilkes Booth & David E. Herold in the Northern Neck of Virginia, April 22-26, 1865* (Clinton, Md.: Surratt Society, 2001), 108-109.

190 See Mrs. Quesenberry's statement to Col. H. H. Wells, cited above. The more or less default account of the meeting between Mrs. Quesenberry and Herold is Tidwell, Hall, & Gaddy, *Come Retribution*, 5, 457-58. See also, Michael W. Kauffman, "Booth's Escape Route: Lincoln's Assassin on the Run," *Blue & Gray Magazine*, 7 (June 1990), 40, and his *American Brutus: John Wilkes Booth and the Lincoln Conspiracies* (New York: Random House, 2004), 297-98.

191 Just exactly whom Herold talked to is a mystery. Mrs Quesenberry related the story by saying "my daughter," in her statement of the Statement of Elizabeth Rousby Quesenberry given to Union Provost Marshal Colonel H. H. Wells, May 16, 1865. Mike Kauffman said Alice was Herold's kibitzer in "Booth's Escape Route: Lincoln's Assassin on the Run," 40 but, after being corrected by living Quesenberry relative, called her Lucy in his *American Brutus*, 297-98, see Michael W. Kauffman to William L. Richter, July 16, 2008, in authors' possession. Stewart avoids the issue, introducing Miss Duncanson, the governess, as the chief character who handled things until Mrs. Quesenberry arrived, *Confederate Spies at Large*, 120. Using the notion that Mrs. Quesenberry's three younger children were under the care of the older girls leaves Louisa and Lucy and Miss Duncanson. We have chosen stepdaughter Louisa, the eldest, as the one who confronted Herold for artistic reasons—she advanced the story we wished to portray. See Joseph E. "Rick" Smith III and William L. Richter, *In the Shadows of the Lincoln Assassination: The Life of the Confederate Spy Thomas Harbin* (Laurel, Md.: Burgundy Press, 2008), 123-27. We maintain our consistency here.

federate Army signalman, Private Joseph N. Baden, Jr., both of whom who lived in the old plantation school house nearby. Harbin cautioned Mrs. Quesenberry not to get too closely involved with the sleeping youth, who proved to be David E. Herold, the companion of the fleeing Lincoln assassin, John Wilkes Booth.[192]

After rousing David Herold and listening to his pleas, which included the use of a horse for his lamed companion, left behind on Gambo Creek about a mile away, Mrs. Quesenberry refused him any assistance. According to one historian, a frustrated Davy Herold then blurted out what no one wanted to hear: "The man who is with me killed Abe Lincoln and is within a mile of this house." A horrified Mrs. Quesenberry peremptorily ordered him off her property.[193]

As the dejected Herold withdrew, Thomas Harbin, who pretty much already knew that Booth had to be the missing man, suggested that she make up a basket of food that he would take to the two fugitives and then send them down the line to other Confederate agents, who would hie them along in making their escape. Before he had gotten out of earshot, Mrs. Quesenberry called out to Herold telling him to leave a trail and she would send him and his companion something to eat presently. Davy's spirits must have been raised with this good news.[194]

After dinner, Harbin took the food basket and disap-

---

[192] A fuller story than those sources in note 8 above (which we follow with some modification, e.g., we do not believe that Harbin and Baden cleaned Herold up as the young Nick Quesenberry said in later years, in our In the Shadows of the Lincoln Assassination, 123-27) is in Stewart, Confederate Spies at Large, 120-22. But the best and most complete account is by local historian, John F. Stanton, "Mrs. Quesenberry and John Wilkes Booth." *King George Journal*, May 2008, who posits that Booth and Herold were looking for a spy camp once run by Pliney Bryan on Gambo Creek and got lost unitil a free Black, Ol' showed Herold the way to The Cottage.

[193] Stanley Kimmel, *The Mad Booths of Maryland* (2nd rev. and enlarged ed., New York: Dover Publications, 1969), 239.

[194] James Swanson, *Manhunt: The 12-Day chase for Lincoln's Killer* (New York: HarperCollins, 2006), 259, errs in saying that Mrs. Quesenberry gave to food directly to Herold.

peared for a what Mrs Quesenberry described as "half an hour," although it was probably much longer. Harbin reported that he had fed the two men and taken them over to William Bryant, a farmer and Confederate sympathizer who lived a mile north of the Cottage. Bryant was to take them by horseback to another Rebel of note with a long arrest record of aiding the Southern cause, Dr. Richard Stuart. *Of course*, Mrs. Quesenberry tried to report the presence of the two strangers to the authorities by hailing Federal gunboats patrolling the Potomac, but none had answered her signals. She was so isolated that she had no other way by which to alert Federal authroities. Curiously, she also said that she had heard that Booth and Herold had crossed the Rapahannock at Port Royal after leaving Stuart's Cleydael house.[195]

Sometime in mid-May, after Booth's death at Garrett's Farm, Federal soldiers arrived to arrest Mrs. Quesenberry and Private Baden, Harbin having earlier disappeared with a price on his head from all of his wartime activities. Mrs. Qusenberry was allowed to stay with her children at the old family home, Rosedale, and was released after making her sworn testament on May 16.

Why was she let go? One historian speculates that the Federals has enough people on trial for aiding Booth and Herold more directly or for having knowledge of their plans ("I told him he must go away," she told her interrogator), that there was one female prisoner on trial (Mary Surratt) fated to hang already, and Mrs. Quesenberry was too pretty to prosecute, or perhaps too well-connected. As famed Union newspaper writer George Alfred Townsend would remark later, "she would have been a superior woman anywhere." But punishment would come for

---

[195] As Edward Steers, Jr., *Blood on the Moon: The Assassination of Abraham Lincoln* (Lexington: University of Kentucky Press, 2001), 185, points out, for an allegedly innocent, know-nothing woman, Mrs. Quesenberry was up on a lot of information she could only obtain from still-active Confederate agents in the field like Harbin.

Elizabeth Rousby Quesenberry in another form. Her daughter Lucy, traumatized by her mother's arrest, sickened and died in 1865 before the family removed to Texas with Alice's new husband four years later.[196]

---

[196] Stewart, *Confederate Spies at Large*, 122, Townsend quote on 117. For Lucy's death, and for the fate of others touched by Lincoln's assassination, see Kauffman, *American Brutus*, 398.

VIII.

"Behold! I Tell You a Mystery"

Who Was Mr. Crismond?[197]

A Mr. Chrisman was mentioned only once in all of Lincoln Assassination lore. Dr. Richard H. Stuart invoked his name during the statement he gives to the federal authorities on May 6, 1865. In his statement, Dr. Stuart said, in part:

> I reside in King George County, Va. I have resided there all my life. On Sunday, April 23rd, I had been at tea with my family & had just concluded when someone was announced at the door. I went to the door and found two men brought up by Mr. Bryant & a Mr. Chrisman came with them. They were on horseback I think the smallest one was on the ground when I saw them. It was after dark. I asked, "Who are you?" Said he, "We are Marylanders in want of accommodations for the night." I said, "It is impossible, I have no accommodations for anybody." [198]

Mr. Chrisman. Who was he? Why did he accompany John Wilkes Booth, David E. Herold, the "assassinators" of President Abraham Lincoln, and William L. Bryant, a local farmer and

---
197 The quote is from I Corinthians 15:51 (ESV Bible).
198 Dr. Richard H. Stuart Statement, in William C. Edwards and Edward Steers, Jr., *The Lincoln Assassination: The Evidence*, 1201-1203, quote on 1201.

possibly a Confederate agent who was a member of the underground apparatus working in King George County, Virginia, in bringing the two men up to Dr. Stuart's? This is a mystery indeed.

This perplexity is increased by the fact that there was a multitude of Crismonds (not Chrisman as the Union military or civilian stenographer put it) in King George County. But it is mitigated somewhat because there are only two families of Crismonds that seem relevant to Dr. Stuart's statement—that of Henry R. Crismond and that of Cadwallader Crismond.[199]

Henry R. Crismond became the person of interest for renowned Lincoln Assassination researcher and writer, historian James O. Hall. The first to look into who the Crismond was who accompanied Lincoln assassin John Wilkes Booth, his traveling companion David E. Herold and their guide, William Bryant to Dr. Stuart's door that April 23, Hall came to the conclusion it had to be family patriarch, Henry A. (as he incorrectly labeled him) who was the correct Crismond, who led the small cavalcade to Stuart's summer home Cleydael. Because of its location several miles back from the Potomac, Stuart stayed there throughout the war to avoid Federal naval raiding parties (slaves stealers, as the Southerners saw them) and the occasional shelling by river gunboats (although his riverside home, Cedar Grove miraculously managed to avoid that misfortune).[200]

Hall believed, although he could not definitively prove it, that Richard Crismond was Stuart's overseer on the latter's 154-

---

[199] In addition to the Henry Crismonds and Cadawalader Crismonds, for example, there is a Lorenzo Crismond living where the Machodoc turns south, west of the Quesenberry's The Cottage Plantation, but he is 17 years old in 1860 and ruled out because of youth and being a ward of 77 year old Edmund Hooms. Federal Manuscript Census, Free Persons, 1860, Ancestry.com.

[200] Michael W. Kauffman, *American Brutus: John Wilkes Booth and the Lincoln Conspiracies* (New York: Random House, 2004), 298.

slave plantation of 3,000 acres.[201] At least the census takers listed Crismond's occupation as overseer. For whom he worked is unknown, but, according to the Federal census takers, he and his family lived right next door to Stuart's Cleydael in 1860. After the war, he moved to Chotank, near Stuart's normal pre-war winter home, Cedar Grove, on the Potomac, before returning to his 1850 haunts in Caroline County across the Rappahannock during the 1870s. Evidently he no longer was in the employ of Stuart, emancipation having made his job superfluous.[202]

Like historian Hall, modern-day assassination expert Michael W. Kauffman also focused on Henry R. Crismond; this time, however, he believed that his son, John L., a much younger man, to be the proper party of concern. He, too, is listed as an overseer in the 1860 Federal census, the only one in which he was of age, even though he lived at home.[203]

Using his usual methodical methods of research, Kauffman went into King George County and walked the ground, scouting the areas around Cleydael, marking building sites, and even noting changes in the old structure's interior, and locating the good doctor's examining and waiting rooms off the back entrance. Twenty-one-year-old John Crismond was much more likely to be out in the cold after dark with strangers than his fifty-two-year-old-father. But as Kauffman admitted recently, "it's not definitive."[204] Like the elder Crismond, John wound up

---

201 Excerpts from Stanley Kimmel papers, Merle Kelce Library, Tampa, Fla., typescript complied by Michael W. Kauffman, September 7, 1985, and copied for the James O. Hall papers, James O. Hall Library, Surratt Society, Clinton, Md.; Federal Manuscript Census, Free Persons and Slave Schedule, 1860, Ancestry.com.

202 Federal Manuscript Census, Free Persons, 1840, 1860, 1870, 1880, Ancestry.com.

203 Federal Manuscript Census, Free Persons, 1860, Ancestry.com.

204 Michael W. Kauffman to William L. Richter, January 11, 2013, email in hard copy, in author's possession. Also full of "might haves" but more certain in its conclusion, nonetheless, that the Crismond involved was John, is the article by King George County historian, John F. Stanton, "Another Look at Crismond," *Surratt Courier*, 38 (No. 4, April 2023), 3-5.

south of Cleydael in Edge Hill, Virginia, after the war, with his occupation listed as farmer.[205]

And so the matters stood until the authors of this essay found another likely Crismond. Federal Census records show that a Cadwallader Crismond resided in King George, Virginia and that he was listed in residence and as head of a household in 1840, 1850, 1860 and 1870, until his death on June 3, 1877 in King George County. He is listed by census enumerators variously as Cad, Cadd, Cadwallader and Cadwalada, but always with the surname of Crismond.[206]

Cad Crismond was born about 1811 at King George, Virginia. His parents' names are unknown. On April 25, 1836, at age 25, he married Frances Jones at King George. On November 7, 1844, at age 33, he married Ann Nancy Sullivan at King George. On September 24, at age 38, he married, for the last time, Louisa Rollins at King George. Louisa would survive Cad and be listed in June of 1880 as living still at King George in the Potomac District, suffering with rheumatism.[207]

Crismond's occupation was also listed variously between 1850 and 1870 as either "farmer" or "overseer." His personal wealth was reported as being between $350 and $675 and the value of his real estate was listed as being between $1,500 and $1,600 during the same period. According to the 1850 Slave Schedule, he owned but three slaves, one female and two male.[208]

---

205 Federal Manuscript Census, 1870, Ancestry.com.
206 Cad Crismond, Federal Census, Free Persons, 1840, 1850, 1860 and 1870, Ancestry.com.
207 Louisa Crismond, Federal Census, Free Persons, 1880, Ancestry.com.
208 Cad Crismond, Federal Census, Free Persons, 1860, Slave Schedule, 1850; Nicholas & Elizabeth Quesenberry, Federal Census, Free Persons, 1860, Ancestry.com; John Stewart, *Confederate Spies at Large: The Lives of Lincoln Assassination Conspirator Tom Harbin and Charlie Russell* (Jefferson, N.C.: McFarland Co., Inc., 2007), 114-16. See also, Joseph E ."Rick" Smith III and William L. Richter, *In the Shadows of the Lincoln Assassination: The Life of Confederate Spy Thomas H. Harbin* (Laurel, Md.: Burgundy Press, 2007), 71-74.

The above is all very interesting, but now, to return to the original question; why was Crismond in company with William Bryant, John Wilkes Booth and David Herold? There were two probable reasons.

When Booth and Herold arrived at Gambo Creek, Herold set out to find "The Cottage," a plantation owned by the widowed Mrs. Elizabeth Quesenberry, who had been mentioned to them by Thomas Jones, their spy handler and member of the Confederate Secret Service up in Maryland.[209] When Mrs. Quesenberry saw Herold, she sent him away. But as the disappointed Herold left, she sent Confederate spy coordinator Thomas Harbin, who lived at an abandoned schoolhouse on the Quesenberry plantation, after him to get Booth on his way south. Finding Booth with a broken leg, Harbin got a hold of William Bryant, who had several horses, to take them to Dr. Stuart's on the way to Port Conway for the night.[210]

But the instructions to Cleydael were a mite confusing to one who did not know the narrow-lane Virginia dirt roads, often mere tracks through the woods. Harbin told Booth and Herold to take the back roads to get to Dr. Stuart's Cleydael. The pathway led to St. Paul's Episcopal Church, a small rectangular brick building and a turn in the road called "Union" by the local slaves. But Booth and Herold had never been in this part of Virginia and feared that they might get lost in the rapidly approaching darkness. So Harbin told them that William L. Bryant would act as their guide.

But by the time Bryant got his charges to St. Paul's darkness was fast advancing. He became confused as to which road was the one to Cleydael. But he knew someone who could show them

---

209 John M. and Roberts J. Wearmouth, *Thomas A. Jones: Chief Agent of the Confederate Secret Service* (Port Tobacco, Md.: Stones Throw Publishing, 1995), who include a copy of Jones' 1893 book, *J. Wilkes Booth . . .* , with the relevant material on 130-31 (109-10 of Jones' story).

210 Smith and Richter, *In the Shadows of the Lincoln Assassination*, 128-32.

all the way. Just behind St. Paul's lived Cad Crismond. Bryant quickly enlisted Crismond in their sojourn to Dr. Stuart's.[211]

Bryant explained that Dr. Stuart's wife was a distant relative of General Robert E. Lee and the doctor had been arrested for suspected pro-Confederate activities and held in the Old Capitol prison in Washington, D.C., for most of May 1863, until he was acquitted of all charges and specifications by a Federal court martial in June.[212] Harbin knew that Stuart would not relish harboring suspicious men claiming to be escaped prisoners of war, especially if they were brought in by Bryant, a lower-class, possibly mulatto, farmer living with a black woman who was, nominally, his wife.[213]

This is where Cadwalader Crismond came in, once again. It is not known for whom he acted as an overseer before the war, but the suspicion is that it was the Quesenberrys. In July 1860, Crismond's household was enumerated on the same census page as the household of Elizabeth's now dead husband, Nicholas Quesenberry. Hence Crismond seems to have had an entrée to the planter class that a simple farmer of mixed race, such as Bryant, would have lacked.[214] Contrary to the historical stereo-

---

211 Excerpt from Kimmel papers, Kauffman typescript, explains the roads upon which Bryant took Booth and Herold and where they founbd Crismond at St. Paul's Church. See also copy of wartime map of King George County Virginia, graciously presented to the authors by John F. Stanton, during a personal guided tour of King George County, March 19, 2012.

212 Excerpt from the Kimmel papers, Kauffman typescript. See also, hand-written notes by James O. Hall on Dr. Stuart's imprisonment, James O. Hall papers, James O. Hall Library.

213 For Stuart, Harbin, Bryant and the transport of Booth and Herold southward to Stuart's home Cleydael, see William A. Tidwell with James O. Hall, and David Winfred Gaddy, *Come Retribution: The Confederate Secret Service and the Assassination of Abraham Lincoln* (Jackson: University Press of Mississippi, 1988), 457-60. A more dramatized presentation is in William L. Richter, *The Last Confederate Heroes: The Final Struggle for Southern Independence & the Assassination of Abraham Lincoln* (2 vols., Laurel, Md.: Burgundy, 2008), II, 242-51.

214 The race of persons enrolled in the Federal Census was a matter of the observation of the census taker or personal knowledge or statement of the enrolled. It was highly subjective. Bryant was listed in no Federal Census before the war, although he was a freeman. His race comes from the Federal Manuscript Census for 1870, Ancestry.com, which shows him as a mulatto carpenter from Virginia living along with his black wife, also from Virginia, in a black slum along upper 7th Street in Washington, DC. For that matter John L. Crismond is listed as a free mulatto in the 1860 Federal Manuscript Census, but white otherwise.

type, an overseer of the white race, like Crismond, was not necessarily an out-cast from plantation society, but an accepted and valued member of the planter society.[215]

So, "a Mr. Crismond" came along to lead the way in the dark night and give an endorsement, a surety in effect, as to Booth and Herold's Confederate *bona fides*. Whether he was a part of the Confederate underground and what role he may have had in the Rebel Secret Service is not known. But as soon as he arrived, he disappeared from the pages of history as fast as he had entered them, another shadowy figure of what historian David W. Gaddy aptly named the "Gray Cloak and Dagger."[216]

---

[215] The overseer has a bad reputation with plantation owners and their spouses in Southern history, see James Oakes, *The Ruling Class: A History of American Slaveholders* (New York: Knopf, 1982), 24, 156, 174-75; Catherine Clinton, The *Plantation Mistress: Woman's World in the Old South* (New York: Pantheon, 1982), 191. This is challenged in William Kauffman Scarborough, *The Overseer: Plantation Management in the Old South* (Baton Rouge: Louisiana State University Press, 1966), 3-19, 158-77, 195-201. A general discussion of planters, their wives and overseers is in William L. Richter, *Historical Dictionary of the Old South* (Lanham, Md.: Scarecrow, 2006, second enlarged edition forthcoming in March 2013), 258-59, 267-69.

[216] David W. Gaddy, "Gray Cloak and Dagger," *Civil War Times Illustrated*, 14 (July 1975), 20-27; *id.*, "Confederate Spy Unmasked: An Afterward," *Manuscripts* (30 (Spring 1978), 94.

IX.

"I SHALL SHOOT MYSELF THROUGH THE HEAD"

Could John Wilkes Booth Have Committed Suicide at Garrett's Farm?

It is a familiar story told repeatedly by historians. Early on the morning of April 26, 1865, noted actor John Wilkes Booth, the man who assassinated President Abraham Lincoln, was shot while in a blazing tobacco barn on the farm of Richard Garrett near Port Royal, Virginia. Rescued from the fire by the Union cavalrymen who had pursued him, Booth was removed to the Garrett's front porch where he died just after dawn, paralyzed below the neck, his nerves severed by the bullet that had passed through his cervical spine, asphyxiated by the fluids that his failing heart could no longer remove from his lungs.[217]

Even before Booth died, the question arose as to who killed him. History tells us it was Sergeant Boston [born Thomas

---

[217] Francis Wilson, *John Wilkes Booth: Fact and Fiction of Lincoln's Assassination* (Boston: Houghton Mifflin Co., 1929), 180-82; Michael W. Kaufman, *American Brutus: John Wilkes Booth and the Lincoln Conspiracies* (New York: Random House, 2004), 321-23; Edward Steers, Jr., *Blood on the Moon: The Assassination of Abraham Lincoln* (Lexington: University of Kentucky Press, 2001), 203; James L. Swanson, *Manhunt: The 12-Day Chase for Lincoln's Killer* (New York: HarperCollins, 2006), 334-35, 339-40; Bill O'Reilly, *Killing Lincoln: The Shocking Assassination that Changed America Forever* (New York: Henry Holt and Co., 2011), 275-76.

Rob Wick, "Why Did Everton Conger Burn Down Richard Garrett's Tobacco Barn?" *Surratt Courier*, 33 (May 2008), 6-7, theorizes that Col. Everton Conger was suffering from old war wounds on the extended ride to find Booth and wanted to get it over with posthaste. While not disagreeing with this analysis, we think that the fear that more Federal forces might arrive soon and dilute the reward money also had great influence in hastening the denouement.

H.] Corbett from Company L of the 16th New York Volunteer Cavalry.[218] A self-castrated religious mystic, Corbett came forward ("Who fired that shot?") and told his commanding officer and the two civilian detectives with him, that he fired contrary to orders to take Booth alive, because he believed that Booth was about to shoot one of them. As Corbett succinctly put it: "Providence directed my hand."

But did He? Or did the Almighty direct some other "hand" to commit the deed? Evidently Confederate spy Thomas H. Harbin voted for the delegated approach. When he intercepted the fleeing Booth near "The Cottage," the Virginia plantation owned by Mrs. Elizabeth R. Quesenbery on Williams Creek, Harbin warned Booth, "John, you will not be able to get very far. The Government is hunting you on all sides. They will capture you, or shoot you."

"No, they will never capture me," Booth retorted. "I shall shoot myself through the head with this." He displayed a 44 cal. Colt's Army revolver to drive home his threat.[219] Harbin was not alone in his belief that Booth committed suicide. Lt. Byron Baker and Lt. Col. Everton Conger, the two detectives from Col. Lafayette C. Baker's National Detective Police leading the cavalry patrol, thought so. Each accused the other of shooting Booth, even though they could not see each other when the shot was fired. Conger then concluded that Booth might have shot himself. Baker demurred and opined that the man who shot Booth ought to go back to the District under arrest for violating

---

[218] On Boston Corbett, see Richard F. Snow, "Boston Corbett," *American Heritage*, 30 (June-July 1980), 48-49; and Laurie Verge, "The Killer of John Wilkes Booth," in Michael W. Kauffman (ed.), *In Pursuit of . . . : Continuing Research in the Field of the Lincoln Assassination* (Clinton, Md.: The Surratt Society, 1990), 111-12. Corbett's own intriguing tale is in Steven G. Miller (ed.), "Boston Corbett's Long-Forgotten Story of Wilkes Booth's Death," *Surratt Courier*, 26 (May 2001), 5-7; *ibid.*, 26 (June 2001), 4-6.

[219] *Cincinnati Enquirer*, August 3, 1884.

orders. Despite Corbett's confession as to being the shooter, he was not arrested. Indeed, he became a hero.[220]

But the actual account is not as simple as modern commentators would like us to believe. As pointed out by historian H. Donald Winkler, there are at least four scenarios that could have taken place at the Garrett's tobacco barn.[221] First, Booth shot himself. No one really examined Booth's weapons to see if one of the revolvers had been fired, even though Baker had to twist one revolver from the fallen actor's hand. Booth had told Willie Jett, one of the Confederate soldiers who brought him to Garrett's, that he would not be taken alive to be marched through Washington like some Roman captive from centuries before.[222] Others who are against this theory point out that Booth had a carbine in his right hand and a crutch under his left arm. But Col. Conger said that Booth had thrown down the crutch and

---

220   U.S., 40th Cong., 1st Sess., 1867, *House Reports*, No. 7/2, "Impeachment: Testimony before the Judiciary Committee of the House of Representatives in the Investigation of the Charges against Andrew Johnson," 323-33, 479-90. A good summary of the "Impeachment Testimony" as regards the shooting of Booth and the pursuers' response is William L Reuter, *The King Can Do No Wrong* (New York: Pageant Press, 1958), 43-51. One of the best accounts, unfortunately unpublished, is Jeanine Clarke Dodels, "The Last Days of John Wilkes Booth," 15-28.
   The number of sources commenting on the death of Booth includes but is not limited to Jacob Mogelever, *Death to Traitors: The Story of General Lafayette C. Baker, Lincoln's Forgotten Secret Service Chief* (New York: Doubleday & Company, 1960), 357-60; Roy Z. Chamlee, Jr., *Lincoln's Assassins: A Complete Account of their Capture, Trial, and Punishment* (Jefferson N.C.: McFarland & Company Inc., Publishers, 1990), 155-57; Theodore Roscoe, *Web of Conspiracy* (Englewood Cliffs, N.J.: Prentice-Hall, 1959), 387-98; Osborn H. Oldroyd, *Assassination of Abraham Lincoln: Flight, Pursuit, Capture, and Punishment of the Conspirators* (Washington: O. H. Oldroyd, 1901), 70-78; Laughlin, Clara E. *Death of Lincoln: The Story of Booth's Plot, His Deed and the Penalty* (New York: Doubleday, Page & Co., 1909), *Death of Lincoln*, 147-53; George A. Townsend, *Life, Crime, and Death of John Wilkes Booth*, 32-39; Michael W. Kauffman, "Booth's Escape Route: Lincoln's Assassin on the Run," *Blue and Gray Magazine*, 7 (June 1990)[Special Issue], 49-50; Mason, "A True Story of the Capture and Death of John Wilkes Booth," 127-39; David Rankin Barbee, "Lincoln and Booth" (Unpublished ms. in the David Rankin Barbee papers, Georgetown University), 959-84, *passim*, DRB papers, GU.

221   Donald Winkler, *Lincoln and Booth: More Light on the Conspiracy* (Nashville: Cumberland House, 2003), 189-93.

222   Ingraham, Prentiss (ed.), "Pursuit and Death of John Wilkes Booth," *The Century Magazine*, cited in Steven G. Miller, "Death of an Assassin: Homicide, Suicide, or Something Else," in Lincoln-Assassinztion.com, splash page. The full citation is: *The Century Magazine*, 39 (No. 3, January 1890), 443-49, with Booth's desire not to be taken alive and Confederate Lt. M.B. Ruggles' belief that Booth killed himself rather than be captured on 446.

had the carbine in both hands. The only weapon inspected after the fight was the carbine, which was done at Secretary Stanton's bidding. It was found to have a cartridge jammed in its breech.[223] Hence Booth's desperate need for a properly functioning weapon casts doubt on Private Emory Parady's statement that the actor was too loaded down with extraneous items in his hands to have committed suicide.[224]

Second, some thought that Conger was the one who shot Booth under orders from Union Secretary of War Edwin McMasters Stanton. He and Baker argued the point at the door when Conger returned from starting the fire that eventually gutted the barn. But how could Conger have shot an upright Booth in such a manner as to cause the bullet to travel downward through the neck, unless Booth was bent over?[225] The same problem faces us in the third scenario, that Corbett shot Booth. Again, to achieve the proper trajectory, Booth had to be bent over sideways from the waist. He was an athlete, not a contortionist. There is also another problem with the theory that Corbett made the shot. Researcher Col. Julian E. Raymond, a combat veteran of World War II, maintains that Corbett and the other troopers were armed with carbines, not pistols. Booth was wounded by a ball fired from a .44 caliber handgun as opposed to the standard .52 caliber carbine round.[226]

Fourth, it is possible that someone completely unrelated to the pursuing Federals shot Booth. Winkler believes that Booth

---

223 William L. Reuter, *The King Can Do No Wrong*, 47, 53-55.

224 Quoted in Steven G. Miller, "Death of an Assassin: Homicide, Suicide, or Something Else," in Lincoln-Assassination.com, splash screen, as of Feb. 28, 2012. Miller has looked at approximately 55 accounts of the shooting at Garrett's farm and finds Parady's story to be the only independently and marginally reliable (in our estimation, not Miller's) one beyond Corbett's own self-serving tale. Miller to Richter, November 26, 2011, e-mail in the author's file.

225 Reuter, *The King Can Do No Wrong*, 46-51.

226 Robert A. Fowler, "Album of the Lincoln Murder: Illustrating How It Was Planned, Committed, and Avenged," *Civil War Times Illustrated*, 4 (No 4, July 1965), 49.

was headed toward Milford Station to join up with Col. John S. Mosby's command. The three Confederate soldiers who had guided him from Port Royal to Garrett's farm were members of Mosby's command. Another Confederate soldier home from the war, Enoch Mason, had ridden the ferry across the Rappahannock with Booth, his companion David E. Herold, and the three Confederate cavalrymen. Mason had immediately galloped out of Port Royal southward upon landing. The suspicion is that he went to inform Mosby of Booth's presence. Several local boys home from the war were present at dinner at Garrett's the day before Booth was shot. If they were informed of the presence of Union troops on the road past Garrett's, it may have been decided that Booth had to be killed to prevent him from talking and telling all he knew of the plots against Lincoln, be they abduction or assassination.[227]

The most recent approach as regards who shot Booth is an article by Blaine V. Houmes and Steven G. Miller, which asserts that Booth committed "suicide by cop." Not an unheard of concept nowadays, and becoming more popular or perhaps more notable, theirs is the notion that a malefactor unable to commit his own suicide forces the police to shoot by threatening them with a weapon. In Booth's case, if this is so, he becomes one of the first to be so categorized. One does have some misgivings that, given the weapons available in 1865, Booth was taking a great chance at being horribly wounded, which is exactly what happened, rather than instantly killed.[228]

---

227 Besides Winkler's treatment, this is a main thesis of Joseph E. "Rick" Smith and William L. Richter, *In the Shadows of the Lincoln Assassination: The Life of Confederate Spy Thomas H. Harbin* (Laurel, Md.: Burgundy, 2007), 119-40. See also, Kate H. Mason, "A True Story of the Capture and Death of John Wilkes Booth," *Northern Neck Historical Magazine*, 13 (December 1963), 127-39, and J. Sydnor Massey, "Chapter in the Death Chase of John Wilkes Booth," *Richmond Times-Dispatch*, April 12, 1905, reprinted in Lincoln Assassination Discussion, General Category, All Things Lincoln Assassination, Enoch Mason's Story of the Last Days of Booth" (Lincoln-Assassination.com).

228 Dr. Blaine V. Houmes and Steven G. Miller, "The Death of John Wilkes Booth: Suicide

Houmes and Miller are probably correct in theorizing that Booth wanted to commit suicide by cop. Historian James L. Swanson related how Booth dared the Yankees to back off 100 yards and form a skirmish line and that he would come out of the barn and take them all on. Swanson correctly understands the Booth mind-set when he compares this to a Shakespearean drama or perhaps a knight jousting at a medieval tournament, throwing down the gauntlet to any who would accept his challenge, romanticism versus realism. Booth later gallantly halved the distance and offered to do combat at fifty yards. But the Union officers were not about to allow Booth the chance to kill or wound any of their men. Besides, they wanted Booth alive. Secretary of War Stanton had so willed it. In Booth's mind the Union men had no pride, no honor. But the Yankees saw it as a matter of realism versus romanticism.[229]

This stance of the cavalry patrol commanders put Booth in a quandary. He had to surrender and face arrest and an eventual hanging for killing Lincoln. Or he could end the whole thing immediately by committing suicide. It was a choice Booth addressed in a typically Southern fashion—humiliation or honor. These things were important in the Old South—or to medieval England and its chronicler, the playwright William Shakespeare, whom Booth and his neighbors revered.[230]

---

by Cop?" *American Journal of Forensic Psychiatry*, 25 (No. 2, 2004), 25-36. See also, Miller's most recent effort in this matter, "Death of an Assassin: Homicide, Suicide, or Something Else," in the home page to Randal Berry's forum, lincoln-assassination.com, and Miller (ed.), a modernization of James O. Hall, "A Case of Mistaken Identity," in *Occasional Papers*, 1 (no. 1, November 2011), 35-48.

229   James L. Swanson, *Manhunt: The 12-day Hunt for Lincoln's Killer* (New York: Harper Perennial, 2006), 330-31. Rollin G. Osterweis, *Romanticism and Realism in the Old South* (Baton Rouge: Louisiana State University Press, 1967), explains the Southern propensity to romantic callings. For Booth's tendency in this direction, see his letters to T. William O'Laughen in John Rhodehammel and Louise Taper (eds.), *"Right or Wrong, God Judge Me": The Writings of John Wilkes Booth* (Urbana: University of Illinois Press, 1997), 35-44, especially 37-39.

230   Osterweis, *Romanticism and Realism*, 3-57. Booth's challenge to the Federal soldiers is straight out of the Old South and the *Code Duello*. See, *e.g.*, Joanne B. Freeman, *Affairs of Honor: National Politics in the New Republic* (New Haven: Yale University Press, 2000),

In our mind, Booth did that which had to be done. It was already scripted; he had penned it in his diary: "Who can read his fate? God's will be done. I have too great a soul to die like a criminal. Oh, may He, may He spare me that, and let me die bravely." [231] Booth simply decided to blow his brains out. But in throwing down his carbine and crutches and drawing his revolver, he underestimated the weakness of his broken leg and the weight of the weapon's barrel. Instead of shooting himself behind the ear, he stepped forward, wincing in pain and off balance, the barrel sliding down his neck as he fired, mortally wounding himself.

But, all this is debatable theory. The question remains: was Booth physically able to have committed suicide in such a way as to produce the type of wound from which he subsequently died? Noted assassination authority, Dr. John K. Lattimer, makes much of the fact that Booth could not have shot himself, because the "long-barreled" 1860 Colt's Army Model revolver was too heavy for Booth to manipulate to get his thumb on the trigger without using both hands. He was encumbered with the Spencer carbine or his crutch or both in his left hand. Moreover, Lattimer asserts, Booth could not have produced the angle of the bullet's path if he fired the gun with his thumb because his arm being held at his side would have prevented it.[232]

If Booth had tried to shoot himself with his index finger on the trigger, as a handgun is normally held and fired, Lattimer continues, Booth could not have reproduced the proper angle of the shot either. Lattimer made use of photographs to illus-

---

Bertram Wyatt-Brown, *Southern Honor: Ethics and Behavior in the Old South* (New York: Oxford University Press, 1982), and Elliott J. Gorn, "Gouge, Bite, Pull Hair and Scratch: The Social Significance of Fighting in the Southern Backcountry," *American Historical Review*, 90 (1985), 18-43.

231 Rhodehammel and Taper (eds.), *The Writings of John Wilkes Booth*, 155.

232 John K. Lattimer, *Kennedy and Lincoln: Medical and Ballistic Comparisons of Their Assassinations* (New York: Harcourt, Brace, Jovanovich, 1980), 61-84.

trate his point regarding the impossibility of Booth inflicting the wound, which he sustained. In the photos, he has his demonstrator hold the weapon to his head with his elbow held down and close to his side.[233]

If one holds the gun as Lattimer shows one ought, his story is correct. But, that is not the way a skilled shooter would do it. Rather than holding the weapon with our elbow at our side, we held it as any man familiar with firearms, as Booth was,[234] with our elbow out to the side and above our shoulder height. The revolver is held as normal, but with the barrel down and the handgrip up. It is possible in this manner not only to duplicate the angle and trajectory of Booth's wound, but almost any angle one wishes to achieve. The barrel is long, but not *that* long. Again, moving the elbow out away from one's side and holding it at shoulder height or above allows one to produce almost any angle of bullet path. And it can easily be done one-handed, without changing the normal grip on the revolver.

Lattimer also vetoes the notion that Booth could have committed suicide because the autopsy mentioned no powder burns or collateral damage a close shot would incur.[235] He shot pork necks and left them exposed to the elements for thirty hours, just as Booth's body was before autopsy, to reach his conclusion. The problem here is that Booth's decaying body was already blackened and distended so badly that initially the first witness to see him (Dr. John F. May, who had removed the boil or cyst from his neck two years earlier), had trouble identifying his horrible visage.[236] According to the Pima County (Arizona) medical

---
233 Ibid., 79

234 On Booth's familiarity and skill with revolvers, see testimony of Benjamin Barker, War Department Records, Judge Advocate General, National Archives and Records center as excerpted in David Rankin Barbee papers, folder 216, box 4, Georgetown University.

235 Lattimer, *Kennedy and Lincoln*, 78-83.

236 See John F. May, "The Mark of the Scalpel," *Records of the Columbia Historical Society*, 13 (1910), 49-68.

examiner, consulted by us, under the right conditions, the body can blacken within twenty-four hours. It was very warm at the end of April 1865, and Booth's body was already in bad shape later on the day he was killed.

With humid weather, as in Virginia and Maryland, a dead body would tend to swell with retained fluids as it decays. Body decomposition does alter the shape and character of wounds. And it is also quite possible that experienced surgeons like Barnes and Woodward did not mention any marks of suicide, such as powder burns, not because they missed them, but because that is what Secretary of War Stanton instructed them to do. Further, forensic professionals say that gunpowder tattooing is left only when the weapon is not in contact with the skin. In any case, the possibility of suicide is neither ruled in nor out in the autopsy reports. As to the assertion that Booth's collar would have caught fire had he shot himself, one wonders if a gun barrel pressed tight to the body (see our photograph) might absorb such fire. Maybe his shirt had no collar (shirts made with detachable collars were a typical style of the time) to catch fire. It is another one of those things that was not mentioned in the autopsy reports. But Congressman and author David M. DeWitt emphasizes that Col. Conger thought that Booth "had the appearance of a man who put a pistol to his head and shot himself—shooting a little too low."[237]

According to Lt. Baker,[238] Booth no longer had the carbine, just a revolver in his hand, when Baker entered the barn after the shot rang out. Indeed, Baker said he had to twist the six-shooter out of Booth's iron grasp. But a man shot through the spinal cord as Booth had been (according to the autopsy report

---

237 David Miller DeWitt, *Assassination of Abraham Lincoln* (New York: Macmillan, 1909), 90.

238 Lattimer, *Kennedy and Lincoln*, 75.

of Dr. J. Janvier Woodward, of the Army Medical Museum),[239] would not be able to hold anything.[240] According to the Pima County Medical Examiner, under the conditions described in the autopsy reports, Booth immediately would have been completely paralyzed from the neck (fourth vertebrae) down, as Barnes had reported. He would not have been rigid, but completely flaccid in his muscles and nerves—nothing functioning as it should. Booth would have dropped anything he was holding as the bullet severed his spinal cord. Lt. Baker either lied or exaggerated, possibly wanting to look like a daring man of action, or more worthy of a bigger share of the reward.

Regardless of whether Booth shot himself or someone else shot him, many, from Confederate Lieutenant M.B. Ruggles, one of those who took Booth to Garrett's Farm, to modern historians, Stanley Kimmel and Larry Starkey, questioned whether Sgt. Corbett actually did it.[241] Oddly enough, Boston Corbett himself never mentioned that he shot Booth in chatty note to a friend named Andrew, a letter written on May 1, 1865, five days after the alleged shooting took place.[242]

Corbett's letter notwithstanding, others saw it otherwise. Otto Eisenschiml concludes that Conger shot Booth to stop him from incriminating Stanton or other unnamed persons of note, connected to the Federal government, in Lincoln's assassination.[243] We doubt that, but the fact remains that Booth was

---

239   *Ibid.*, 69-70.

240   See also, the autopsy report of Surgeon General J. K. Barnes, in Laurie Verge (ed.), *The Body in the Barn: The Controversy Over the Death of John Wilkes Booth* (Clinton, Md.: The Surratt Society, 1993). 67-68.

241   Ingraham, Prentiss (ed.), "Pursuit and Death of John Wilkes Booth [Ruggles' story]," 446; Stanley Kimmel, *The Mad Booths of Maryland* (Indianapolis: Bobbs-Merrill, 1940), 257 (text), 364-65 (fns. 55-61); Larry Starkey, *Wilkes Booth Came to Washington* (New York: Random House, 1976), 146-49, especially 147.

242   See Richard Sloan, "Remembering a Lincoln Assassination Collector," *Surratt Courier*, 35 (No. 3, March 2010), 8. Richard Sloan to William L. Richter, August 15, 2012, e-mail in author's files, for the details of the letter which Sloaan found at an auction.

243   The best narrative of what happened at Garrett's Farm is Jeannine Clarke Dodels, "The

physically able to produce the wound that Lattimer maintained he could not. But we agree, as one investigator says in Lattimer's study, if Booth shot himself, he did it in the back of the head to save his pretty face.[244] As he raised the weapon to fire the shot which would take his life, his hand slipped and the shot cut his spinal cord instead of blowing his brains out—a final blow of the ill-fortune that had plagued all of his endeavors against Lincoln since January 1865.

The point of this study is just this: that it was absolutely possible for Booth to have shot himself in the manner we describe. Did he keep his promise to Thomas Harbin and end his own life? No one knows. Did Corbett shoot Booth as he maintained? No one knows. And there the story must remain. The witnesses *saw* nothing; but everyone *heard* the shot. Historians and commentators may believe whatever they choose, but no one can prove anything except Booth died from a bullet through the cervical spine that produced paralysis, and, ultimately, his death.

It has been the contention of historian and Lincoln Assassination scholar, William Hanchett, that we should accord Booth the "respectability of rational political motivation." Booth, Hanchett suggested, "deserves a measure of respect we so generously and indiscriminately pay to men on both sides of the war who fought, killed, and died for what they believed. When we

---

Last days of John Wilkes Booth at the Garrett Farm" (Unpublished and undated paper in the hands of Smith and Richter), who adopts the Corbett story without question. See also, Otto Eisenschiml, "Who Shot Booth?" in *O. E.: Historian Without an Armchair* (Indianapolis: Bobbs-Merrill, 1963), 159-66. Eisenschiml's theory has gone "viral" since its inception; see Fowler, Robert H. "Was Stanton behind Lincoln's Murder?" *Civil War Times*, 3 (Aug. 1961), 4-13, 16-23; and David Balsiger and Charles E. Sellier, Jr., *The Lincoln Conspiracy* (Los Angeles: Schick Sunn Classic Productions, 1977). The *Lincoln Conspiracy* was also made into a television special and a full-length movie.

244 Lattimer, *Kennedy and Lincoln*, 75.

are able to make this concession to Booth," Hanchett concluded, "we will truly understand how terrible the Civil War was."[245]

Perhaps, one hundred and fifty years later, that time has finally come.

---

245 Hanchett, *John Wilkes Booth and the Terrible Truth about the Civil War*, 34-35.

X.

WHY COULDN'T WE HAVE GOTTEN AN AMERICAN FOR THE JOB?

Congressional Supremacy, the Radical Republicans, and the Impeachment of Andrew Johnson

PART 1:
FROM WASHINGTON TO LINCOLN

John Wilkes Booth's assassination of President Abraham Lincoln still haunts our political history today, even as it has been consigned to a brief, often barely mentioned, almost esoteric interlude between the grand eras of Civil War and Reconstruction.[246] It is mentioned in passing in most history classes; studied by a few dedicated buffs and historians whom many dismiss unfairly as mere antiquarians. But it was not always so. Lincoln's administration of the U.S. Government and his death continued to affect American government for years after his assassination.[247]

It all revolved around who would reconstruct the restored Union, the President or Congress, so a little background is called for. In our modern age the notion that a President ought

---

246 James M. McPherson, *Battle Cry of Freedom: The Civil War Era* (New York: Oxford University Press, 1988), 852; Eric Foner, *Reconstruction, 1863-1877: America's Unfinished Revolution* (New York: Harper & Row, 1988), 75.

247 This is a central theme in Thomas DiLorenzo, *The Real Lincoln: A New Look at Abraham Lincoln, His Agenda, and an Unnecessary War* (Roseville, Ca.: Prima Publishing, 2002).

to rule and badger Congress through presidential decree and position papers is not as controversial as it was in the nineteenth century. The nineteenth century was still too close to the rule of the colonies by the prerogatives of the King of England. The colonies broke from what they thought to be excessive executive power with the Declaration of Independence. Thus our first national constitution was the Articles of Confederation, where our President was a non-entity elected by Congress from its own membership, in effect, the executive committee chairman. All power rested with the unicameral Congress, each state having one vote. The individual states were even more assertive of legislative power in their own constitutions.[248]

The result was government on all levels that operated inefficiently, if at all.[249] It was no accident that the Federalists, mostly former Continental Army officers (centralists like George Washington and Alexander Hamilton) who sought to amend the Articles of Confederation, turned out to be counterrevolutionaries who wrote an entirely new document. This Constitution of 1789 increased federal power through a more powerful president and split up the legislative body into a bicameral Congress to weaken the power of the states.[250]

The new Constitution was sold to the American people through the *Federalist Papers* (propaganda written by Hamilton, John Jay and James Madison), which falsely promised that the new document was as respectful of states' rights as the Articles.

---

248 John Fiske, *The Critical Period of American History* (Boston: Houghton Mifflin, 1897), challenges the abilities of the government under the Articles; Jackson Turner Main, *The Sovereign States, 1775-1783* (New York: New Viewpoints, 1973), looks at state government.

249 Merrill Jensen, *The New Nation: A History of the United States during the Confederation, 1781-1789* (New York: Vintage, 1950), questions the inadequacies of government under the Articles.

250 Forrest McDonald, *Novus Ordo Seclorum: The Intellectual Origins of the Constitution* (Lawrence: The University Press of Kansas, 1985); M. E. Bradford, *Original Intentions on the making and Ratification of the United States Constitution* (Athens: University of Georgia Press, 1993).

Opponents of the new Constitution (like Thomas Jefferson, John Hancock, Patrick Henry, and George Mason) were condemned as Anti-Federalists, backward-looking men in favor of a weak country susceptible to un-American English and French influences.[251]

The rift continued after the ratification of the Constitution, made possible by the first ten amendments to further limit Federal power (at the insistence of Mason), and the Federalists carefully buying the votes of still reluctant states with cold cash and political sops (Hancock was falsely promised the presidency to win over Massachusetts), and threatening laggard Rhode Island with blockade and war.[252] Political parties formed around the scope of the new federal power—the Federalists (Washington, Hamilton, and John Adams) in favor, the Democratic-Republicans (no relation to later anti-slavery Republicans) for the old-time state political power. Madison changed from being for the centralized Constitution he helped write and joined Jefferson and his New York ally, Aaron Burr, against its expanded executive powers. But when the Jeffersonians gained power in 1800, each side reversed its position, seeking to deny full national political power to the other.[253]

As newer states, western and southern, joined the Union, the Federalists found themselves a minority political party confined to New York and New England. Almost everyone became a Democratic-Republican in response to the War of 1812 (even John Quincy Adams, son of a Federalist icon who had served

---

[251] Jackson Turner Main, *The Anti-Federalists: Critics of the Constitution, 1781-1788* (Chicago: Quadrangle Books, 1961).

[252] Forrest MacDonald, *E Pluribus Unum: The Formation of the American Republic, 1776-1790* (Boston: Houghton Mifflin, 1965), for a different than usual view on the deals made to get the Constitution ratified.

[253] Stanley Elkins and Eric McKitrick, *The Age of Federalism: The Early American Republic, 1788-1800* (New York: Oxford University Press, 1993) for the politics of this era. See also, an interesting analysis of the changing Constitution in Jill Lepore, "The Commandments: The Constitution and Its Worshippers," *The New Yorker,* 86 (January 17, 2011), 70-76.

as our second President), and, in its aftermath, the Democratic-Republicans came to adopt the concept of massive Federal governmental powers, the exact opposite of their stance in 1800.[254]

In 1820 and 1824, the Democratic-Republicans ran unopposed (the so-called Era of Good Feelings) so few Federalists were left. But not all Democratic-Republicans believed that the new philosophy was for the best, resulting in a party split. They were led by Martin Van Buren, whose front man was Andrew Jackson, and who envisioned a new party based on decentralized government that he would call the American Democracy.

But the winning presidential candidate in 1824 was John Quincy Adams, as close to an old-time Federalist as one could be, minus the name. He joined with Speaker of the House of Representatives Henry Clay of Kentucky, who also had Federalist economic leanings. He called his policy the American System, which would be the centerpiece of Republican political platforms in the latter part of the nineteenth century. Adams and Clay united in a "corrupt bargain" to deny an electoral college majority to the real anti-federalist, Andrew Jackson, who had received a popular vote majority. It was the first presidential election to be decided in the House.[255]

Jackson was hopping mad, as only he could be. He and his followers joined in a four-year campaign to unseat Adams, which they did in 1828. His opponents, angry that the Jacksoni-

---

[254] The first American political system is discussed in Joseph Charles, *The Origins of the American Party System* (New York: Harper & Row, 1961); William Nisbet Chambers, *Political Parties in a New Nation: The American Experience, 1776-1809* (New York: Oxford University Press, 1963). For the dirty tactics endemic to American Politics, see Jill Lepore, "Party Time: Smear Tactics, Skullduggery, and the Debut of American Democracy," *The New Yorker*, 82 (September 17, 2007), 94-98.

[255] On the second American party system, whose prime architect was little-known President Martin Van Buren, see Robert V. Remini, *Martin Van Buren and the Making of the Democratic Party* (New York: Norton, 1970); Richard P. McCormick, *The Second American Party System: Party Formation in the Jacksonian Era* (Chapel Hill: University of North Carolina Press, 1966); and for the downfall of the preceding political system, Norman K. Risjord, *The Old Republicans: Southern Conservatism in the Age of Jefferson* (New York: Columbia University Press, 1965).

ans had grabbed the name the American Democracy for themselves, and that Jackson tended to rule by fiat, called themselves Whigs. This indicated that they were against "King Andrew of Veto Memory" as much as the original Whigs (Patriots) of the American Revolution were opposed to the king-like powers of old George III.[256]

But the Whigs had a hard time electing Presidents. William Henry Harrison died after a month in office, John Tyler switched to the Democrats and annexed Texas, Zachary Taylor died after two years in office, and Millard Fillmore or Henry Clay just plainly could not win a national presidential election. So the Whigs developed the notion of Congressional Supremacy. This meant that the President ought to be subordinate to the wishes of Congress, where all the real Whig leaders of importance resided. Ideally, U.S. senators and representatives could be instructed, in turn, on how to vote by the members of their state legislatures or residents of their congressional districts back home.[257]

In the mid-1850s, in response to the failure of the Wilmot Proviso (no slavery in the territory obtained from Mexico in the recent war) and the passage of the Kansas-Nebraska Act (which repealed the Missouri Compromise of 1820 and opened the entire West to slavery through popular sovereignty), the Northern Whigs and Northern anti-slavery Democrats combined to create the Republican party that would put Abraham Lincoln in office in 1861. Since the Republicans had so many old-line Whigs in their ranks, and the Democrats controlled the presidency during the 1850s through Franklin Pierce and James Buchanan, Con-

---

[256] For the Whigs, see E. Malcolm Carroll, *Origins of the Whig Party* (Durham: Duke University Press, 1925); George Rawlins Poage, *Henry Clay and the Whig Party* (Chapel Hill: University of North Carolina Press, 1936); Arthur Charles Cole, T*he Whig Party in the South* (Gloucester, Mass.: Peter Smith, 1962).

[257] For Congressional Supremacy, see William L. Richter, *The ABC-Clio Companion to the American Reconstruction, 1862-1877* (Santa Barbara, Ca.: ABC-Clio, 1996), 100-101.

gressional Supremacy became an immediate Republican Party staple.

At the same time, the Southern Whigs (predominately in Maryland and Louisiana) went over to the pro-slavery Democrats.[258] The party lines were now drawn for the miniature pre-Civil War of Bleeding Kansas (1854-1861) won by the anti-slavery forces; the John Brown Raids (anti-slavery terrorist forays in 1856 Kansas and 1859 Virginia); Lincoln's loss to Stephen A. Douglas in the famous debates for the Illinois senatorial election of 1858, which revealed Lincoln's potential to lead the party); the election of Lincoln as President (1860); secession of the lower (Gulf) South (1860-1861), and the Civil War (1861-1865). But Republicans could be smug, because in 1860 they had won the presidency and control of Congress with the secession of the South.[259]

---

258 The realignment of the two political parties can be followed in Roy Franklin Nichols, *The Disruption of the American Democracy* (New York: Macmillan, 1948); Kinley J. Brauer, *Cotton Versus Conscience: Massachusetts Whig Politics and Southwestern Expansion 1843-1848* (Lexington: University of Kentucky Press, 1967).

259 William L. Richter, *Historical Dictionary of the Old South* (Lanham, Md.: Scarecrow Press, 2006), 61-63, 155, 200-207, 215-17, 234-35, 253-56, 263-64, 271-72, 277, 287-95, 365-66, 373-74. See especially the introduction, 1-29, which explains the Southern political mind before during secession and during the War of Northern Aggression. For a comprehensive study of the North-South struggle, see William W Freehling, *The Road to Disunion* (2 vols., New York, Oxford University Press, 1990-2007).

Shorter, more specific studies include Richard H. Brown, "The Missouri Crisis, Slavery, and the Politics of Jacksonianism," *The South Atlantic Quarterly*, 65 (Winter, 1966): 55-72; Robert Pierce Forbes, *The Missouri Compromise and Its Aftermath: Slavery and the Meaning of America* (Chapel Hill: University of North Carolina Press, 2007); Freehling, *Prelude to Civil War: The Nullification Controversy in South Carolina, 1816-1836* (New York: Harper & Row, 1965); Chaplain W Morrison, *Democratic Politics and Sectionalism: The Wilmot Proviso Controversy* (Chapel Hill: University of North Carolina Press, 1967); Holman Hamilton, *Prologue to Conflict: The Crisis and Compromise of 1850* (New York: Norton, 1964) who points out that Stephen A. Douglas was probably more responsible for the Compromise than Henry Clay as a recent biographer admits, Robert V. Remini, *Henry Clay and the Compromise that Saved the Union* (New York: Basic Books, 2010); The Kansas Missouri Border Wars are detailed in James A Rowley, *Race and Politics: "Bleeding Kansas" and the Coming of the Civil War* (Philadelphia: Lippincott, 1969).

But nothing beats Arthur Bestor's lengthy study of the South's political philosophy that led to Northern defeat during the 1850s in the Kansas-Nebraska Act and the Dred Scott case in the U.S. Supreme Court than the classic "State Sovereignty and Slavery: A Reinterpretation of Proslavery Constitutional Doctrine, 1846-1860," Illinois State Historical Society, *Journal*, 53 (1960), 117-80.

Unfortunately, the party had reckoned without considering the political timber of their new leader, Abraham Lincoln. The just-elected President refused to call the Congress into session as the war began. He quickly declared war and called up the militia (causing the Upper South to secede); accepted ninety-day volunteers from the several states, expanded the size of the Regular Army and Navy; established new American rules for war through General Orders No. 100, Adjutant General's Office; created an illegal blockade of the South (under international law); denied the writ of habeas corpus (allowed under Congress' powers in the Constitution); threatened to execute Southern privateers as pirates; emancipated slaves within the Confederacy,; and transferred funds between the several executive branches of government without proper appropriation to pay for it all.[260]

Although it was enraged at this executive display of illegal and unconstitutional power, Congress saw no way around it—when it finally came into session it would have to pass a law endorsing every action Lincoln took. The U.S. Supreme Court would follow suit, approving Lincoln's executive decisions until after the war. But the political battle between the executive and legislative branches of the Federal government had just begun. It would be the primary issue in the war and the reconstruction that followed.

---

260 Richter, *Historical Dictionary of the Civil War and Reconstruction* (2nd ed., Lanham, Md.: Scarecrow Press, 2012, soon to be reissued in a second revised edition), 240-43. For congressional approval of Lincoln's executive actions, see David Herbert Donald, *Lincoln* (New York: Simon & Schuster, 1995), 305, arguably the best one-volume study of the sixteenth President to date.

Part 2:
Reconstruction

Congressional Supremacy Writ Large

While the Republican-controlled Congress was more than willing to endorse President Lincoln's use of the executive proclamation to advance the Union war effort, it angered Republican legislative leaders that their roles had been reduced to being rubber stamps for the executive. Lincoln jumped at the opportunity to cooperate in their passage of the 1860 party platform, essentially Henry Clay's economic program, the American System, and Lincoln, as Clay's outspoken Whig acolyte for years, was more than willing to grace measures like the National Banking System, high protective tariffs, land grant colleges, and the Union Pacific railroad with his presidential signature. Congress saw this as Congressional Supremacy in action.

But party leaders wanted more. They wanted to set the policy for the reconstruction of the reunified nation—bringing the wayward South back into the Union with a new Constitution purged of all of the evils that prewar Southern society represented. These vices included slavery; white planter supremacy in state governments; the alleged degradation of non-slaveholding white farmers (called "plain folk" by modern historians or condemned as "po' white buckra" by enslaved blacks who took on the airs of their wealthy owners); and the lack of a productive factory-based economy in favor of staple agriculture. But most of all, the most malefic was the Slave Power Conspiracy, the Southern domination of the Federal Government by control of the presidency. Lincoln would be the only Northerner to be elected to two terms in the first eighty-seven years of the nation's history, and only the third elected president openly and morally opposed to slavery after the Adamses, John and John Quincy). The slave-holding South also controlled Congress through committee assignments and the counting of 3/5 of the slaves for representation even though they could not vote, and the Supreme Court through appointment (two of the five pre-Civil War chief justices were Yankees, meaning slave owners John Marshall of Virginia and Roger B. Taney of Maryland dominated the bench for 64 years, right on through the Civil War).

Hence the North had wanted to reconstruct the South and the Union long before the powder smoke and report of the first shot fired on Ft. Sumter had dissipated. Republicans, and certain "War" Democrats in Congress, saw secession and the battlefield conflict as their golden opportunity and Congressional Supremacy as their weapon of choice to expand the theory and practice of American democracy.[261]

Oddly congressional Democrats, not Republicans, made the first attempts to reconstruct the nation during the secession crisis. In separate plans, senators R.M.T Hunter of Virginia and Stephen Douglas of Illinois suggested that some sort of economic alliance be drawn up that provided for common foreign policy, tariffs, trade regulations, patents, and copyright laws. All domestic institutions like slavery were to be state functions except that slavery was to be guaranteed in the territories until statehood whereupon any new state could prohibit it

---

261 Eric Foner, *Free Soil, Free Labor, Free Men: The Ideology of the Republican Party before Reconstruction* (New York: Oxford University Press, 1970); Frederick J. Blue, *The Free Soilers: Third Party Politics, 1848-1854* (Urbana: University of Illinois Press, 1973). Some notion as to dates of Reconstruction and how they have changed from the traditional (Kenneth M. Stampp, *The Era Of Reconstruction, 1865-1877* [New York: Vintage, 1967]; William A. Dunning, *Reconstruction: Political ands Economic, 1865-1877* [New York: Harper Bros., 1907]) to the more modern (W. E. Burghardt DuBois, *Black Reconstruction, . . . 1860-1880* [New York, Harcourt Brace, 1935]; Harold M. Hyman [ed.], T*he Radical Republicans and Reconstruction, 1861-1870* [Indianapolis: Bobbs-Merrill, 1967]; Eric Foner, *Reconstruction: America's Unfinished Revolution, 1863-1877* [New York: Harper & Row, 1988]).

(popular sovereignty), basically Chief Justice Taney's Dred Scott decision. But these plans all recognized secession and Congress rejected them.[262]

The minute Lincoln refused to give up Southern forts, the North, in effect, occupied Confederate territory and could reconstruct it, come what may. Beginning in 1861, various Northern agencies ranging from the Army to the Treasury Department to private reconstruction organizations to various religious denominations flooded the occupied South to purify it. Starting around Fortress Monroe in the Virginia Peninsula, then New Orleans, the southeastern third of Louisiana and the Mississippi Valley north through Mississippi and Arkansas to Memphis, Tennessee, the process went forward in a disjointed fashion, freeing slaves (declared contraband of war), seizing cotton (to pay for the war) and managing abandoned plantations (putting freed slaves to work under U.S. Army supervision, and saving souls).[263]

But this was all icing on the cake. The real reconstruction was to be political. It was here President Lincoln and his Republican Party came to blows over Congressional Supremacy. This was particularly true of Lincoln and his successor, Andrew

---

262 Robert W. Johannsen, *Stephen A. Douglas* (New York: Oxford University Press, 1973), 832-34; Jeffrey J. Crow, "R.M.T. Hunter and the Secession Crisis, 1860-1861: A Southern Plan for Reconstruction." *West Virginia History* 34 (April 1973), 273-90.

263 Foner, *Reconstruction*, 35-76. It is commonplace in the Surratt Society to roundly condemn Leonard F. Gutteridge and Ray A. Neff, *Dark Union: The Secret Web of Profiteers, Politicians, and Booth Conspirators that Led to Lincoln's Death* (New York: John Wiley & Sons, Inc., 2003) in the harshest words (Edward Steers, Jr., and Joan Chaconas, "Dark Union: Bad History," *North & South*, 7 [No. 1, January 2004], 12-30). This may hold for the assassination theories put forth in the book (pp. 69-210), but the corrupt machinations of the various military, religious, benevolent organizations and government officials (pp. 1-68) during early wartime Reconstruction are remarkably accurate. For similar stories of Reconstruction shenanigans, see, *e.g.*, Willie Lee Rose, *Rehearsal for Reconstruction: The Port Royal Experiment* (New York: Vintage, 1967); Louis S. Gerteis, *From Contraband to Freedman: Federal Policy toward Southern Blacks, 1861-1865* (Westport, Conn.: Greenwood Press, 1973); Ludwell H. Johnson, III, *Red River Campaign: Politicians and Cotton in the Civil War* (Baltimore: Johns Hopkins University Press, 1958); and Martha M. Bigelow, Freedmen of the Mississippi Valley, 1862-1865," *Civil War History*, 8 (1962), 38-47.

Johnson, and one branch of the Republican Party, those called the "ultras" or the Radicals.

The Radical Republicans believed in several non-negotiable principles. They thought the newly freed slaves possessed certain civil rights. First of these was the right to vote. Blacks were the only obviously loyal, potentially Republican group in the South. Ironically, the end of the Civil War brought about increased representation to the Southern states because blacks would be counted not as 3/5 of a person but as a whole person.

The Radicals found other civil rights were important, too, like national citizenship previously denied all blacks, slave or free, by the Dred Scott case; the right to own property even though confiscation of Rebel property (the legendary "forty acres and a mule") proved too much for a majority of Civil War era congressmen; the trial of blacks by a jury of their peers; equal protection under the law; and education (to cast an intelligent vote and protect other rights). The South was soon overrun by teachers sent from the North through various religious and benevolent societies. Southerners scoffed at the idea of blacks being educated by these "Yankee School Marms." But at the same time, just in case, nightriders burned schools, assaulted teachers, and terrorized and threatened students.

Although they bestowed citizenship upon the black population, with the rights and privileges that went with it, the Radicals believed that full benefits and rights ought to be denied white Rebels until, guided by Congress, they did penance for their secession and the war. And, most of all, Congress was to be the controlling institution of Reconstruction. The President had a role to perform, but he was to be definitely subordinate to Congress. Congressional Supremacy was the word of the day.

One might be a Radical Republican on some issues and a

moderate or Conservative on others. The balance within the party changed constantly. But all Republicans believed that conditions ought to be placed against automatic readmission of the Southern states back into the Union.

What motivated these Radicals? Revenge (it had been a hard war), political advantage (the South had to have a viable Republican base, the black voter), guarantee of the wartime Republican accomplishments (tariffs, taxes, freedom of slaves), the Pacific railroad out of Chicago, and the National Banking System, all played a part. There was a fear of a lost peace otherwise.

Finally, idealism moved the Radicals; a desire to help freed slaves gain their rights as a freed people, to amend the old Constitution and to make it a "New Birth of Freedom," in Lincoln's words. The Radicals were men of unusual principle not normal in American politicians. In ordinary times they might not have even been elected. As it was, those Republicans from the safest seats in Congress generally were the most radical. As their seats were threatened by Democrat opponents, Radicals became Moderates (for *some* Reconstruction), or if seriously endangered, they became Conservatives (for *little* Reconstruction). But all Republicans agreed with the Radicals to some degree at one time or another.[264]

---

264 T. Harry Williams, *Lincoln and the Radicals* (Madison: University of Wisconsin Press, 1941); Hyman (ed.), *The Radical Republicans and Reconstruction*, xvii-lxviii; Hans L. Trefousse, *The Radical Republicans. Lincoln's Vanguard for Radical Justice* (New York: Knopf, 1969); David H. Donald, *The Politics of Reconstruction, 1863-1867* (Baton Rouge: Louisiana State University Press, 1965), and his "The Radicals and Lincoln," in Donald (ed.), *Lincoln Reconsidered* (New York: Vintage, 1956), 103-27. The standard historical debate on how important the fight between Lincoln and the Radical Republicans was is Donald, "Devils Facing Zionwards," who says it was of little import and Williams, "Lincoln and the Radicals," who argues it was a key inter-party fight. See Grady McWhiney (ed.), *Grant, Lee, Lincoln and the Radicals* (Evanston, Il.: Northwestern University Press, 1964), 72-91, 92-117, respectively.

Part 3:
Lincoln and the Radicals

Political Reconstruction went through three distinct phases: Conservative (Presidential), Moderate (Congress seeking accommodation with the President), and Radical (Congressional Supremacy as put forth by the Radical Republican leadership with increasing support from their more moderate and conservative colleagues). Gradually the cautious Radical beginnings became a torrent of demands endorsed by the Northern voters in the congressional election of 1866 for obedience from the executive and judicial branches of the recalcitrant Yankee government and the defeated but defiant Confederate South to guarantee the results of the Union victory through a more thorough peace process.

Prior to Lincoln's Emancipation Proclamation and employment of black soldiers, the Radicals complained that Lincoln was moving too slowly to defeat the Confederacy through necessary policies. They organized the Committee on the Conduct of the War to speed things up through Congressional Supremacy over domestic policy and removing ineffective generalship (i.e., politically incorrect or non-Republican ideologues) from the battlefield.[265]

But after the Emancipation, the Radicals objected to Lincoln moving too quickly to readmit the wayward South back into the Union. It was time for a strong application of Congressional Supremacy to slow the Reconstruction process. The clash came

---

265 Bruce Tap, *Over Lincoln's Shoulder: The Committee on the Conduct of the War* (Lawrence, Kan.: University Press of Kansas, 1998); E. B. Long, "The Committee on the Conduct of the War," *Civil War Times Illustrated*, 20, (August 1981), 20-27. A good listing of sources on Lincoln and Reconstruction is in David A. Lincove (ed.), *Reconstruction in the United States: An Annotated Bibliography* (Westport, Conn.: Greenwood Press, 2000), 77-81.

after Lincoln introduced his suggested plan of Reconstruction, commonly known as the First Presidential or Ten Percent Plan.

Part of his annual message to Congress, December 8, 1863, the President proposed that whenever ten percent of the population of a seceded state signed an oath of future loyalty to the Union and recognition of the acts of Congress passed since secession, they could elect a constitutional convention to draw up a new state constitution, elect a loyal state government, and send representatives and senators to the U.S. Congress. No mention was made of slavery as Lincoln feared that the Emancipation Proclamation was unconstitutional. Higher officials in the state and Confederate governments were not allowed to participate until later. Finally, the state had to be occupied by Federal troops.

The Radical Republicans went wild. How dare Lincoln act alone without consulting them? Reconstruction was a congressional prerogative under the dictates of Congressional Supremacy. Ten percent? This was an infinitesimal number in any democracy. Where were the demands that the South free their slaves? What was this war for anyhow?

Lincoln called these objections "pernicious abstractions." He, of course, was thinking that he would be lucky to get ten percent of the Confederate white population of any Confederate state to cooperate with him during the war. And he was not going to allow slavery to prolong the conflict. He saw emancipation as a gradual process, lasting to 1900 and beyond. Like Henry Clay before him, Lincoln envisioned the colonization of American slaves to a place in Latin America (called Lincolniana by wags) or back to Africa (American created Liberia) as the ideal means for resolving the "Negro Question." Failing this, Lincoln believed that blacks would be doomed to second-class citizenship in the states, North or South.[266]

---

266 William B. Hesseltine, Lincoln's Plan of Reconstruction (Chicago: University of Chicago

Congress hit back at Lincoln's conservative approach to Reconstruction immediately that summer. Under the leadership of senate Radicals Benjamin Wade of Ohio and Henry Winter Davis of Maryland, Congress passed the Wade-Davis Bill. This called for more severe conditions for readmission of the seceded states. It assumed that if the states were not out of the Union they were so far gone Congress could set special conditions for their readmission to the Union.

According to the Wade-Davis plan, when fifty percent of the 1860 registered voters had taken an oath of future loyalty (the idea was more than democratic—this would postpone Reconstruction until Republicans were better prepared to look at it), the offending state could call a new state constitutional convention. This body had to abolish slavery, disfranchise higher Confederate and state officials, and repudiate the Confederate war debt (the debt made the Confederacy a nation, to repudiate it denied that and the veracity of secession). Then the new state could elect a state government and present representatives and senators to Congress, which might accept them and readmit the state back into the Union. Many Republicans abstained from voting, but it was passed July 2, 1864. Congress then adjourned.[267]

The end of the congressional session meant that President Lincoln could pocket veto the Wade-Davis Bill without comment. But Lincoln spoke out against it anyway. He said he feared that his emancipation provisions were unconstitutional

---

Press, 1967); Peyton McCrary, *Abraham Lincoln and Reconstruction* (Princeton, NJ: Princeton University Press, 1978). Lerone Bennett, Jr., *Forced into Glory: Abraham Lincoln's White Dream* (Chicago: Johnson, 2000), an expansion of his "Was Lincoln a White Supremacist?" *Ebony*, 23 (1968), 35-38, 40, 42, is harshly critical of Lincoln's notions of white supremacy. See also, *ibid.*, 610-15, quoting Lincoln, policy toward free blacks as "root hog or die!" from Hampton Roads Peace Conference. For a much more complimentary approach, see Harold M. Hyman, "Lincoln and Equal Rights for Negroes," *Civil War History*, 12 (1966), 258-66.

267   Herman Belz, *A New Birth of Freedom: The Republican Party and Freedmen's Rights* (Westport, Conn.: Greenwood, 1976), 57-62.

and an amendment was needed to end slavery. But, the President further stated that he preferred not to be limited to any one approach. Should any ex-Confederate state, however, prefer to use the provisions of the harsher Wade-Davis Bill, he would honor their choice.[268]

How typically Lincoln! Clever, slippery, indirect, and to the Radicals, insulting. The Radicals responded with the Wade-Davis Manifesto. It unfairly and inaccurately accused the President of interfering with Congressional Supremacy to forward his own suspicious, milder Reconstruction goals in the South for personal political gain. Indeed, Lincoln spoke out on April 11, 1865 (delivering a speech which some historians believe pushed assassin John Wilkes Booth to the breaking point), saying that it was better to accept his ten percent governments in Louisiana, Arkansas, Tennessee, and Virginia rather than start anew. But he was willing to reconstruct the rest of the South by a Congressional plan. He only suggested that the more intelligent blacks and Negro soldiers who fought for the North receive the right to vote.[269]

PART 4:
JOHNSON AND THE REBELS

For all practical purposes, Reconstruction was unsettled when Lincoln died on the morning of April 15, 1865. Lincoln's successor was his vice president, Andrew Johnson. The Radicals could hardly contain their glee. As U.S. Senator in 1861, Johnson had refused to secede with his home state of Tennessee. He served as the only Democrat on the Committee on the Conduct

---

268 Foner, *Reconstruction*, 61-62

269 Michael W. Kauffman, *American Brutus: John Wilkes Booth and the Lincoln Conspiracies* (New York: Random House, 2004), 209-10.

of the War. He was so staunch a Union man that Lincoln made him military governor of Tennessee under Union occupation. In this most dangerous position, Johnson served with courage, pledging to make "treason odious." He survived several assassination attempts in the meantime.[270]

In 1864, Lincoln wanted to run for reelection, not as a Republican, but as a National Union Party man. War Democrats like Johnson gave Republicans a distinct advantage in local, state and national representation. So Lincoln, upon re-nomination, demanded that Johnson be his running mate. This created quite a stir, even among Republicans who admired the Tennessean. "Can't you get a candidate for vice president without going down into a damned rebel province for one?" groused Pennsylvania's noted Radical Republican, Thaddeus Stevens with contempt.[271] Stevens preferred an "American." But with Johnson's support on the ticket, Lincoln became the first Northerner to gain a consecutive second presidential term in the nation's history.

In the wake of Lincoln's death, as his Radical compatriots crowded around Johnson to congratulate him ("Johnson, we have faith in you. By the gods, there will be no trouble in running the government!" Radical Ben Wade crowed), few knew that Stevens' doubts about the new executive would prove dismayingly correct. After all, Johnson had reassured the Radicals who praised him, "Treason must be made infamous, and traitors must be impoverished."[272]

But as much as the Radicals praised Johnson, he was no Republican by any stretch of the mind. He was named after Andrew

---

[270] Peter Maslowski, *"Treason Must Be Made Odious": Military Occupation and Wartime Reconstruction in Nashville, Tennessee, 1862-1865* (Millwood, NY: KTO Press, 1978); Hans L. Trefousse, *Andrew Johnson: A Biography* (New York: Norton, 1989). 26. Fawn Brodie, *Thaddeus Stevens: Scourge of the South* (New York: Norton, 1959), 220. A good listing of sources on Andrew Johnson is in Lincove (ed.), *Reconstruction in the United States*, 82-96.

[271] Brodie, *Thaddeus Stevens*, 220.

[272] *Ibid.*, 223.

Jackson and was a life-long Democrat. Although he hated the Southern plantation grandees, their holdings of many slaves, and their secession theories with a passion, he owned slaves himself and saw slavery as a social institution—it kept blacks in their place, more or less segregated from white society. This irked a man like Thad Stevens, who believed in racial equality before the law.

Johnson wasted no time in getting on with Reconstruction, as he saw it. He had been sick with typhoid fever all spring 1865, often took whiskey on an empty stomach, and appeared drunk to observers who did not understand his physical weakness from illness. This was why Secretary of War Edwin Stanton had handled the prosecution of the Lincoln assassins. As usual at times of nineteenth century sectional crisis, Congress was out of session. Like Lincoln before him, Johnson decided not to call a special session. Now hale and hearty, he would get the ball rolling himself.

So Johnson issued the Second Presidential Plan of Reconstruction. He recognized everything that the Lincoln governments had done so far under the Ten Percent Plan. But he issued a series of Presidential Proclamations covering the remaining seven states of the former Confederacy, beginning with North Carolina on May 29, 1865 (the rest were almost exact copies).

In some ways, Johnson utilized parts of the Wade-Davis Bill. But like Lincoln, Johnson assumed that he could use the powers of amnesty and pardon to act without prior congressional approval. That challenged the Republican Congress' predilection for Congressional Supremacy. But Johnson was a Democrat, not a Republican. He moved as Andrew Jackson would have, with executive action. Had not Lincoln done the same?

First, Johnson said a majority of the voters in each state as of 1860 had to take an oath of future loyalty. This was logical as the war was over. Certain high ranking civilian and military men were excluded until pardoned individually. But here Johnson did something different. He also excluded all men worth $20,000 or more, unless they made special, individual application. This hit his old enemies, the plantation owners. They would have to crawl for forgiveness. And they did! They came, they crawled, they begged—and Johnson forgave them all and restored their voting rights and property. There would be no forty acres and a mule for ex-slaves under President Andrew Johnson! Of the estimated 16,000 excluded for wealth, Johnson pardoned 13,500 in no time at all (many of the others refused to humble themselves initially, but most relented later).[273]

Johnson appointed a provisional governor for each state, usually an 1861 Union man. He would supervise the oath-taking process and call a state constitutional convention to draw up a new permanent government. This new government would have to repudiate secession, repudiate the Confederate state debt, and recognize the recently passed Thirteenth Amendment to the U.S. Constitution, abolishing slavery. Then a new state government could be elected along with representatives and senators to Congress.

Each state followed the Johnson proclamation; or if not the entire proclamation, at least a portion of it. Some failed to abolish slavery statewide, but endorsed the Thirteenth Amendment. Others refused to endorse the amendment but abolished slavery locally. Still others failed to repudiate their share of the

---

273 J. T. Dorris, "Pardoning the Leaders of the Confederacy," *Mississippi Valley Historical Review*, 15 (June 1928), 3-21. A lengthy list of the pardoned and their land restorations appears in U.S., 40th Cong., 1st Sess., 1867, *House Reports*, No. 7/2, "Impeachment: Testimony before the Judiciary Committee of the House of Representatives in the Investigation of the Charges against Andrew Johnson."

The Last Shot

Confederate debt. They said it was so intermixed with other debt as to be unrecognizable.

Johnson ignored all of this double-talk and declared them legitimate states once again. In this he did the South a great disservice. He implied not much had to be done to rejoin the Union. He seemed to want to get these states back in Congress where all those Democratic votes would rebound to his advantage. And so, in the end, Johnson wound up supporting the very men he despised, the rich planters. He was too stubborn to admit that he might have erred. Instead of controlling the planters; they now controlled him.[274]

Just how much the old guard in the South controlled Johnson was made apparent immediately, even before Congress came into session. The "Johnson Governments" in the South began passing discriminatory laws, so-called Black Codes, against the newly freed slaves that, depending on the state, restricted their right to serve on juries, their right to bear arms, their right to move freely on the public roads, right to choose or switch to new employers, broadly defined unemployed blacks as vagrants, and compelled them to be available to work all hours of the day or night. Violators were put to work in chain gangs on public works or farmed out to labor pools in a form of quasi-slavery.

At the same time blacks were granted the right to marry, assume a family name, draw up contracts, hold property, sue or be sued, and attend segregated public schools. While the North in general saw these laws as an outrageous violation of freedom, Southern whites had copied these laws from U.S. Army orders employed by occupation troops to preserve law and order.[275]

Unfortunately for the white South, the Black Codes, whether

---

[274] Dan T. Carter, *When the War Was Over: The Failure of self Reconstruction of the South, 1865-1867* (Baton Rouge: Louisiana State University Press, 1985).

[275] Theodore G. Wilson, *The Black Codes of the South* (University, Ala.: University of Alabama Press, 1965).

endorsed by the Army or not, were installed amid a constant backdrop of race riots, in which blacks always sustained more casualties than whites. The disturbances occurred in cities such as Norfolk, Virginia, Memphis, Tennessee, and New Orleans, Louisiana. It took the Federal troops to restore order.[276]

Then as their crowning achievement, Johnson's new state governments called for elections, which produced men called Conservatives, usually of the ex-Confederate variety. Johnson had not made the right to vote available to the former slaves, nor had his new state governments. But the worst of the results was when the Johnson governments sent their new representatives and senators to Congress in December 1865. Only eight months after the end of the worst war in American history (until then) Southerners sent the Confederate vice president, four Confederate generals, five Confederate colonels, six Confederate cabinet officers, and fifty-eight members of the Confederate Congress to represent them in the Union Congress. Not one of these men could have served without a special pardon from President Johnson.[277]

Why did the South do this? Poor judgment comes to mind. But these men were the natural leaders of their states, had contacts from the war and antebellum associations, and would, in many cases, be familiar men for the North to deal with. Many had opposed secession even though they all served the Confederacy. And here the ultimate weakness of Presidential Reconstruction came into play. Congress judges the legitimacy of its own members. The clerk of the house refused to seat these men, or even to call their names during the taking of the roll. The Senate followed in due course with the same policy. Congressional Supremacy now ruled with the aid of the U.S. Constitution.

---

276 Richter, *The ABC-Clio Companion to the American Reconstruction*, 295-99.
277 *Ibid.*, 97-98.

Part 5:
Johnson and the Radicals

The Radical Republicans were very angry at Johnson's Reconstruction results. They saw in it a mockery of the results of the war. Hundreds of thousands had died or been maimed in vain. Yankee visitors to the South reported unrepentant Confederate sympathizers everywhere. But more moderate congressional voices prevailed. The rest of the party thought the situation could be saved if Johnson would agree to certain congressional proposals, meaning, if he would but admit to constant Congressional Supremacy.

When Congress met in December 1865, it quickly established a Joint Committee of Fifteen on Reconstruction to show the way.[278] It was obvious that the Southern notion that they had lost the war and ought to be readmitted immediately without conditions was out. So was the Presidential Theory, presented by Lincoln and Johnson, that the South had never left the Union in the first place and ought to be brought back in with a minimum of demands.

Under Radical Republican theories the Southern states had left the Union or sundered their relationship with the loyal states. Representative Thaddeus Stevens preferred that the seceded states be treated as captured provinces under international law and should be legislated for by the North, in every manner including changing their boundaries. Senator Charles Sumner of Massachusetts theorized that the seceded states had committed a form of suicide and reverted to territorial status. Congress

---

278 John G. Clark, "Radicals and Moderates on the Joint Committee on Reconstruction," *Mid-America*, 45 (1963), 79-98; Richard G. Lowe, "The Joint Committee on Reconstruction: Some Clarifications," *Southern Studies*, n.s., 3 (1992), 55-66. William A. Dunning, *Reconstruction: Political and Economic*, 52, correctly points out that the Committee of Fifteen was an assertion of Congressional Supremacy.

would supervise their recreation of a republican (political theory, not political party) form of government, as it did with all territories before admission to the new Union.

But most of the Republicans preferred that the South be seen as having forfeited their political rights. This meant that any law passed to further the sundering of the Union was null and void from its inception (*ab initio*). All other laws (marriages, birth records, debts, contracts and common everyday matters, like Federal taxes levied during the war) and former state boundaries were valid, but Congress could determine when a state was properly reconstructed by merely seating its representatives and senators (according to the 1840 Supreme Court case, Luther *v.* Borden).[279]

So Congress, through the Joint Committee of Fifteen, led by Senator Lyman Trumbull of Illinois, attempted to find a Moderate compromise with the President by passing laws to assist with Reconstruction. The first measure was the renewal of a Federal relief agency called the Bureau of Refugees, Freedmen, and Abandoned Lands. Created in early 1865 during the war, the Bureau was to coordinate benevolent societies; assist the freed slaves (now called freedmen as opposed to the wartime term, contrabands), feed, clothe, and temporarily house refugees of all races; provide medical care; find employment and regulate the contract labor system; open freedmen's schools; and administer abandoned plantations.

The Bureau had been set up for of the duration of the war plus a period of one year. The war had been over almost a year at this time and Moderate Republicans (and Radicals) thought this might be a nice way to have Congress and the President work under the banner of Congressional Supremacy. Unfortunately, it

---

[279] A good summary of these theories is in Eric McKitrick, *Andrew Johnson and Reconstruction* (Chicago: University of Chicago Press, 1960), 93-120.

seemed that men who worked well with the freedmen could not get along with planters and vice versa. President Johnson vetoed the Renewal Bill as an unconstitutional use of wartime powers in a time of peace, and Congress sustained him by a narrow margin.[280]

Rebuffed, Congress tried another tack. They passed a measure called the Civil Rights Bill of 1866. It was designed to grant a Federal guarantee of citizenship to the freedmen for the first time (negating the old Dred Scott decision). Before this, citizenship had been a state right. The Civil Rights Bill also safeguarded black rights that the states had compromised in the Black Codes. The whole Republican Party was for this. But Johnson was Democrat. He vetoed the measure as an unwarranted interference with states' rights under the Constitution and the Bill of Rights.[281]

That did it. Congress struck back by passing the Civil Rights Act over Johnson's objections. And for good measure it re-passed the vetoed Bureau Bill, too. Then, led by Senator Trumbull and the Joint Committee of Fifteen, Congress decided that the Civil Rights Act was so important that it passed it as the first section of a proposed Fourteenth Amendment to the U.S. Constitution. Other amendment clauses negated the Confederate debt, guaranteed the Union war debt, and provided no compensation for the freed slaves. It also required the black vote in the former Confederate states to offset the increased representation provided for by the freedmen, or reduced the representation for the Southern states in proportion to those disfranchised at state level; and finally, prohibited anyone who had taken an oath to the United States and then to the Confederate States from holding a state or Federal office, until pardoned by Congress.

---
280   *Ibid.*, 274-97.
281   *Ibid.*, 298-325.

The new proposed amendment was sent to the states. The problem was that certain Northern Border Slave States were patently against it. So Congress sent the amendment to all the states, Union or former Confederate. Here Congress faced another dilemma. Was the South in the Union or out? It would take the adverse vote of only ten states to veto the new amendment, if all were counted.

No matter. Of the eleven ex-Confederate states, only Johnson's Tennessee approved of the Fourteenth Amendment.[282] Ten other Southern states rejected it outright, with President Johnson egging them on. Moreover, Johnson began attacking the leading Radicals in public speeches by name.

PART 6:
ASHLEY, BOUTWELL AND THE BEGINNINGS OF IMPEACHMENT

President Johnson probably ought to have been more circumspect in his handling of the Radical Republicans. But he mistakenly thought he was on a roll with the public. This might have been true south of the Mason-Dixon Line and the Ohio River, but it was not so north of this boundary. The Northern public was becoming wary of this Southern former Democrat in the White House.

Nonetheless, Johnson decided to attack his Radical Republican opponents in the open. It was the manly, forthright thing

---

[282] Johnson's arch-rival in Tennessee was the governor, Parson William G. Brownlow, who arrested enough members to obtain a quorum, impeached the speaker of the house when he wavered, and then took a vote, "two of Andrew Johnson's tools not voting. Give my respects to the dead dog in the White House!" See Richter, *The ABC-Clio Companion to the American Reconstruction*, 55-58, 275. For how historians and jurists have viewed the Fourteenth Amendment, see William L. Richter, "One Hundred Years of Controversy: The 14th Amendment and the Bill of Rights," *Loyola [New Orleans] Law Review*, 15 (1968-69), 281-95.

to do. Immediately after the veto of the Freedmen's Bureau Bill Johnson addressed the public for the traditional Washington's Birthday celebration at the national capital. It was an impromptu speech given at the White House. Historically, such ad-lib addresses have a bad way of backfiring on the speaker. This was Johnson's first public speech since the inaugural where he had been sick and slightly drunk. Bourbon never goes well with an empty stomach.

Off-the-cuff speaking was a Southern art form and Andrew Johnson was its past-master. He used the word "I" 152 times and compared his plan of Reconstruction with the type of plan Jesus Christ would have used—kind, just, forgiving. Then he said that there were men in the North who were fully as treasonous as Jefferson Davis "and a long list of others."

"Give us their names," cried an anonymous voice from the crowd. Johnson felt obliged to state who these Yankee traitors were, Representative Thaddeus Stevens, Senator Charles Sumner and abolitionist Wendell Phillips.

"Give it to Forney," replied the unknown voice. John W. Forney was the clerk of the House of Representatives who had refused to seat the Johnson Government men back in December of 1865.

Johnson was really warmed up now. "Some gentleman in the crowd says 'give it to Forney.' I have only just to say that I do not waste my ammunition on dead ducks." Laughter and applause followed.[283]

Congress was not amused. Immediately the House accepted the resolution proposed by "Impeachment Jimmy" Ashley of Toledo, Ohio, for the judiciary committee to make an exploratory investigation into alleged presidential malfeasances and

---

283   Richter, *The ABC-Clio Companion to the American Reconstruction*, 424-25.

issue a report to the whole House. The legislative body agreed in April 1866.[284]

James M. Ashley was a Campbellite Presbyterian, a very strict sect that practiced in the western Appalachians. Fleeing his father's rigorous discipline, Ashley worked riverboats on the Ohio and Mississippi rivers and came to abhor slavery. He joined the Republican Party after leaving the Democrats for the Free Soilers in 1848. He was an active Republican and stood for Congress in 1858 and was elected and reelected four times. Ashley had a notion that every president who had died in office (Harrison, Taylor) had been poisoned by cabals led by their vice presidents (Tyler, Fillmore). Lincoln was no different. Ashley firmly believed that Johnson had led the plot that killed Lincoln to thwart Republican Reconstruction.[285]

Since Ashley was not a part of the judiciary committee, although he attended their public and private meetings and helped plot strategy, the man who took the lead for the Radicals was committee member George S. Boutwell of Massachusetts. A native of the Bay State, Boutwell was a Democrat turned Republican in 1854, over the Kansas-Nebraska Act's repeal of the Missouri Compromise and the opening of all the west to slavery in the territorial stage of government. Coming from an educated family, Boutwell really never went to public or private schools but briefly. Instead, in modern parlance he was "home schooled." He read widely, much as had Abraham Lincoln.

---

284 U.S., 39th Cong., 1st Sess, 1866, *House Reports*, No. 104, "Assassination of Lincoln," 1. For another location of the same document, see *Boutwell Report*, July [28],1866, George S. Boutwell papers, box 175, Manuscripts Division, Library of Congress (copy in James O. Hall papers, JOHRC, Surratt House Museum, Clinton, Md.). See McKitrick, *Andrew Johnson and Reconstruction*, 486-94, for the rationale of the impeachment of Johnson and the several attempts. See also, Foner, *Reconstruction*, 333.

285 285 On James M. Ashley, see Richter, *The ABC-Clio Companion to the American Reconstruction*, 39-39; Clarence E. Carter, "James Mitchell Ashley," in Allen Johnson, *et al.* (eds.), *Dictionary of American Biography* (10 double vols. + 9 supplements, 1964-1981), I, 389-90. Ashley received 53.4% of the vote in his district in 1866, Donald, *Politics of Reconstruction*, 100.

Boutwell became a store clerk at age thirteen. He read during every spare moment; at night, he frequently doused his head in a bucket of cold water just to keep awake and alert. He entered a nearby attorney's office and read law. His scholarly activities were so intense as to adversely affect his health. He eventually entered politics as a Democrat, beginning at school board level. He was defeated as candidate for the legislature the first two times he ran, then won, and served ten two-year terms. He ran for Congress several times unsuccessfully, but devoted much time to being on boards for almost every reform possible. Elected governor in 1851, he served in the Bay State's Constitutional Convention in 1853 with distinction. Boutwell always knew the rules of debate and never spoke in a flippant manner— he was always to the point and in great length, leading him to be characterized behind his back as "the steady wind blowing aft."

Boutwell left the Democratic Party after the convention and switched to the new Republican Party, working mainly through philanthropic organizations for years. He was elected to Congress in 1864 and served until he was made Grant's Secretary of the Treasury in 1869. In Congress, Boutwell was known as a good-looking, dapper kind of man. He had principles and stuck to them. One was the right of freedmen to vote; "suffrage before restoration" became his motto. Andrew Johnson had violated that motto every time he recognized one of his Southern governments and when he vetoed the freedmen's right to vote in the District of Columbia.[286]

---

[286] The best study of Boutwell is Thomas Domer, "The Role of George S. Boutwell in the Impeachment Trial of Andrew Johnson," *The New England Quarterly*, 49 (December 1976), 596-617. The steady wind quote is from Brodie, *Thaddeus Stevens*, 340. For a full biography, see Thomas H. Brown, *George Sewall Boutwell, Human Rights Advocate*. (Groton, Massachusetts: Groton Historical Society, 1989). Several good short biographies of Boutwell can be accessed on any computer search engine. He predicted the impeachment in his article "The Usurpation," *Atlantic Monthly*, 10 (October 1866), 506. He defended his actions years later in his "Johnson's Plot and Motives," *North American Review*, 141 (December 1885), 574ff. He is credited with twenty-three publications during his lifetime at www.ranker.com. Boutwell received 77.3% of

Boutwell's acting as the Radicals point man in the Judicial Committee's investigation made him the man of the hour so far as impeachment went. Diligently he worked to get past the opposition of committee Democrats and Moderate Republicans to bring Johnson to trial. But he had very little to go on. The Boutwell Report made three tenuous points: 1) Captured Union soldiers had been inhumanely treated in Southern prisons; 2) Jefferson Davis and the Confederate Secret Service agents in their Canadian operation were complicit in the assassination of President Lincoln; and 3) the Confederates in Canada were employed as secret agents or spies. The committee recommended that Jefferson Davis be brought to trial for treason and other crimes and that the executive departments of the United States continue to look into the matter.[287]

The minority report, written by A. J. Rogers, a Democrat representative from New Jersey, essentially scoffed at the paucity of evidence presented by the Republican majority. Rogers complained that he had only been allowed a brief look at materials that the majority had used, but that glance showed that Boutwell had no real facts to back up his report, which relied on the falsehoods perpetrated upon the committee by Sandford Conover, in reality Charles A. Dunham, a notorious con artist. Indeed, Conover, calling himself James Watson Wallace, had once issued a public complaint against himself as Conover, as an "infamous and perjured scoundrel." Rogers also complained that a Radical Republican newspaper editor credited by the committee had stated, "Would that the hand of Booth had been less steady, that

---

the vote in his district in 1866, Donald, *Politics of Reconstruction*, 101.
287 U.S., 39th Cong., 1st Sess, 1866, *House Reports*, No. 104, "Assassination of Lincoln," 3, 8, 10, 29.

of Atzerodt [the drunken, accused killer of Johnson who had failed to act] more sure."[288]

The committee voted 5-4 to do nothing as regarded impeachment. Buoyed by the results, Johnson went on to actively campaign against the Radical Republicans in the fall congressional elections. The Radicals sent delegations a day or two after Johnson, each side badmouthing the other in turn. The Republicans not only won re-election, they won by a two-thirds majority in both houses. The Northern public was now on the side of the Radicals.[289]

PART 7:
MILITARY (RADICAL) RECONSTRUCTION AND IMPEACHMENT

The Radicals were not about to wait a year for seating the first session of the new veto-proof Fortieth Congress. They struck in the Lame Duck second session of the old Thirty-ninth Congress, using the 1866 Congressional Election as leverage. Immediately upon convening, Congressman Ashley introduced into the House another resolution to impeach President Johnson for treason and high crimes and misdemeanors against the United States. It failed passage.

Then in January 1867, Johnson vetoed a bill to extend the vote to freedmen in the District of Columbia. Capitalizing on renewed Republican anger, Ashley quickly reintroduced his resolution and Congress voted for it, assigning the investigation to the Judiciary Committee. By now, Republicans of all stripes

---

288 *Ibid.*, 30-41. The standard work on Conover is Carman Cumming, *The Devil's Game: The Civil War Intrigues of Charles A. Dunham* (Urbana: University of Illinois Press, 2004).

289 The committee vote is in William A. Dunning, *Essays on the Civil War and Reconstruction* (New York: Macmillan, 1897), 257; for the election, see McKitrick, *Andrew Johnson and Reconstruction*, 421-47.

were convinced that there would be no adequate Reconstruction until the President was out of the picture. Had they succeeded in removing the President (it took four tries to get an indictment and trial) many historians believe that the United States would have approached a parliamentary system with legislative ascendancy or, as the Republicans would have put it, Congressional Supremacy.

As the House Judicial Committee took testimony, the whole House introduced Radical Reconstruction to the nation. They first passed an act to call the Fortieth Congress into session right after the Thirty-ninth would adjourn in March. There would be no more periods when Congress was out of session during which time the President might act without their supervision. Then they enacted the Command of the Army Act that said that the President could give no orders to troops in the field without approval of the Commanding General Lt. Gen. U. S. Grant, already a known advocate of Congressional Supremacy.

Next, Congress passed the Tenure of Office Act that said that any official appointed with advice and consent of the Senate could not be removed without the same advice and consent. This was to protect Secretary of War Edwin McM. Stanton, a Radical spy in Johnson's cabinet, whom he had inherited from Lincoln. Then, Congress put the United Sates Army in charge of administering Reconstruction, even though no martial law was declared. This is why Radical Reconstruction is also called Military Reconstruction.

There were four Military Acts. The first divided the unrepentant South (less Tennessee) into five military districts. Army commanders of the military district, along with the subordinate commanders of each state, were to "assist" the Johnson Governments to do the correct thing, politically. All persons who could not hold office under the Fourteenth Amendment were declared disfranchised. All black males were declared voters. Registrars, appointed and supervised by the Army, were to enroll all voters, who took an oath of future loyalty.

These loyal voters were to elect a state constitutional convention that would draw up a new state constitution, disfranchising all unpardoned whites and guaranteeing the vote to all freedmen. A state could disfranchise more whites if they chose, but the new black voters and representatives refused to do so, except in Louisiana, Arkansas, and Alabama. After the new state constitution was approved by all voters, a new, "more efficient" state government could be set up, the Fourteenth Amendment would be approved and representatives and senators sent to Washington, where Congress would consider seating them.[290]

Meanwhile the House Judiciary Committee moved forward with a new impeachment investigation, whose authority was renewed on March 7, 1867. Ashley's impeachment resolution charged President Johnson with misuse of his appointing power (putting ex-Rebels in charge of the South), misuse of his pardoning power (letting the biggest traitors off the hook and being paid for it), corruptly disposing of U.S. property (returning abandoned plantations to their white owners or heirs), misuse of the veto power (not permitting Congressional Supremacy), and corruptly interfering with elections (speaking out in public against individual congressmen). Some wanted to throw adultery into

---

[290] James E. Sefton, *The United States Army and Reconstruction, 1865-1877* (Baton Rouge: Louisiana State University Press, 1967), 107-211. The Fortieth Congress handled the enforcement of the Reconstruction Acts. The Second Military Reconstruction Act allowed the Army to call the Convention process into action when the Johnson governments refused, the Third declared the Johnson governments illegal and allowed the voting registrars to decide if oaths were taken in good faith, and the Fourth declared that a majority of those voting as opposed to a majority of those registered would be sufficient to pass the new constitutions. Modern historians like to diminish the Army's key role in favor of national and local politicians, sticking with the term Radical Reconstruction. See Foner, *Reconstruction*, 228-79; Kenneth M. Stampp, *Era of Reconstruction*, 83-118.

the mix, but this failed when one wag wanted to know if that were a high crime or a misdemeanor.[291]

But the witnesses really had little beyond disagreeable policies to disagree with Johnson on. Nothing impeachable in that. But this time, the Committee found some interesting things about Lincoln's assassination that did not involve Johnson. First, Booth's captured diary was missing numerous pages; how many and of what import depended on who was testifying.[292] Second, the day of the assassination, Booth's friend and fellow actor John Matthews had received a letter from Booth intended for Editor John Coyle of the *National Intelligencer* newspaper in Washington. Upon hearing of the killing of Lincoln, Matthews had burned the letter. Boutwell drilled Matthews several times to see who might have signed the missive, but the actor could only remember Booth, Louis Payne (Lewis T. Powell), George A. Atzerodt, and David E. Herold. Matthews swore that John Surratt, Jr., was not among them.[293]

Boutwell thought that the lack of pursuit of Surratt since the spring 1865 was an intentional oversight only recently made up for by his arrest, extradition from the Papal States, and trial, on-going concurrently with the impeachment investigation. Sur-

---

291 U.S., 40th Cong., 1st Sess., 1867, *House Reports*, No. 7/1, "Impeachment: Testimony before the Judiciary Committee of the House of Representatives in the Investigation of the Charges against Andrew Johnson," 1-2, has the charges and communication between the members of the committee. The adultery charge may have had more meat to it than anyone imagined at the time. According to one report circulating around Nashville, and not revealed until forty years later, Johnson not only cheated upon his wife with two "soiled doves" who were sisters, but he did so in partnership with none other than John Wilkes Booth. See Hamilton Gay Howard, *Civil War Echoes: Character Sketches and Secrets* (Washington: Howard Publishing Company, 1907), 84.

292 U.S., 40th Cong., 1st Sess., 1867, House Reports, No. 7/2, "Impeachment: Testimony before the Judiciary Committee of the House of Representatives in the Investigation of the Charges against Andrew Johnson," 32-33, 324-25, 449-50, 457-58, 484.

293 On the Matthews letter and its various historical interpretations, see William L. Richter, *Sic Semper Tyrannis: Why John Wilkes Booth Shot Abraham Lincoln* (Bloomington, Ind.: iUniverse, 2009), 149-57.

ratt's eventual salvation through a hung jury did little to improve Boutwell's view of the issue.[294]

Finally, in November 1867, Congress met earlier than the traditional first Monday in December. The idea for an early meeting was Boutwell's. He had wanted to convene the body on or about October 1, but Moderates had balked. Nevertheless, Boutwell had an ace in the hole. He had convinced one member of the Judiciary Committee, John Churchill of New York, to switch his vote to recommend impeachment. The whole House still dithered, hoping Johnson would come to his senses and recognize Congressional Supremacy.

Johnson stubbornly refused to give in. In February 1868 he removed Secretary of War Stanton in direct violation of the Tenure of Office Act. The Senate voted censure. Boutwell saw to it that the House voted to impeach (indict) Johnson for committing high crimes and misdemeanors. This time there were no generalities that would hold Moderates back. There was an actual "crime."

But Boutwell saw high crimes and misdemeanors as more than a mere violation of the law. It was a political charge, filled with great import for the nation's future. He wanted Congressional Supremacy installed for all time through Johnson's conviction by the Senate sitting as a jury. So did Thaddeus Stevens. "If we don't do it," Stevens thundered, "we are damned to all eternity. There is a moral necessity for it," Stevens continued, "for which I care something; and there is a party necessity for

---

294 U.S., 40th Cong., 1st Sess., 1867, *House Reports*, No. 7/2, "Impeachment: Testimony before the Judiciary Committee of the House of Representatives in the Investigation of the Charges against Andrew Johnson," 490, 782-88. On Surratt, see William L. Richter, *Confederate Freedom Fighter: The Story of John H. Surratt and the Plots against Lincoln* (Laurel, Md.: Burgundy, 2007); Andrew C. A. Jampoler, *The Last Lincoln Conspirator: John Surratt's Flight from the Gallows* (Annapolis: Naval Institute Press, 2008); Richter, *Sic Semper Tyrannis*, 45; Domer, "The Role of George S. Boutwell in the Impeachment and Trial of Andrew Johnson," 599-600.

it, for which I care more." Then Stevens admitted the truth, "In fact the party necessity is the moral necessity. . . ."[295]

Following Stevens' lead, Boutwell insisted that the President had no right to remove Stanton merely to test the law in court because he was sworn to see all laws were faithfully executed. He compared Johnson unfavorably to the most notorious impeached offenders in history and insisted that Johnson's acquittal would be "impossible." In his arguments Boutwell, as well as the other House managers, was so intemperate in his remarks as to damage the case against Johnson. Johnson's lawyers merely stuck to the facts and left the hyperbole to the Radical Republicans. The result was the president's acquittal by one vote.[296]

PART 8:
CONGRESSIONAL SUPREMACY TRIUMPHANT

Although Johnson was not found guilty, the Radicals won anyway. For the rest of the nineteenth century, a slew of ineffective presidents served (can you name them?), allowing Congressional Supremacy to reign supreme. Not until Theodore Roosevelt came to power because of William McKinley's assassination did the pattern change. Aptly, McKinley, a major in the 23d Ohio Volunteer Infantry, was the last of the Civil War veterans to serve as president. The sad heritage of Abraham Lincoln's assassination had passed. Roosevelt and Woodrow Wilson introduced a new legacy for the century that followed—one dominated by strong presidents not Congress, and through that legacy, historians would remember Abraham Lincoln as a

---

295 Quoted in Brodie, *Thaddeus Stevens*, 350.
296 The best source in presenting impeachment from Boutwell's point of view is Domer, "The Role of George S. Boutwell in the Impeachment and Trial of Andrew Johnson," 606-17. A good listing of impeachment sources is in Lincove (ed.), *Reconstruction in the United States*, 96-103. Those who voted for acquittal were the old, who could retire, and the young, who could start over. Had any of them balked, there were several more votes available.

strong president, one of the greatest power artists as executive the nation had known.[297]

However, that was all in the future. In 1869, as he left office, just to stick it to the Radical Republicans once more, Andrew Johnson pardoned those Lincoln assassination co-conspirators still alive in prison, Dr. Alexander Mudd, Samuel Arnold, and Edman Spangler. But for Andrew Johnson, the plaintive cry of Thad Stevens still rings out from the past: "Couldn't we have gotten an American for the job?" Finally, they did. His name was U. S. Grant. And he believed in Congressional Supremacy.[298]

The last shot had been fired, both physically and politically. Abraham Lincoln was dead at last. With him went the concept of the peremptory executive proclamation—for four decades. But it had taken a lot more than John Wilkes Booth's bullet to finish the job that made Congress supreme branch of government for the next thirty-five years, as it had been in the Articles of Confederation back in 1781, until the advent of Theodore Roosevelt. Reconstruction may have failed in the South, but it was a success in making the United States "are" into the United States "is."[299]

---

297 See, *e.g.*, the most recent of this genre, Bill O'Reilly and Martin Dugard, *The Killing of Lincoln: The Shocking Assassination that Changed America Forever* (New York: Henry Holt & Co., 2011).

298 David L. Wilson, "Ulysses S. Grant and Reconstruction," *Magazine of History*, 4 (Winter 1989), 47-50.

299 The best and most recent statement of this notion is actually in a novel. See Steve Berry, *The Lincoln Myth* (New York: Ballentine Books, 2014), especially y"131-35, 170-73, 301, 420, 484-87.

CPSIA information can be obtained at www.ICGtesting.com
Printed in the USA
BVOW08s1340241215

R6659600001B/R66596PG430223BVX1B/1/P